KAUA'I
MILE BY MILE GUIDE
The Best of the Garden Isle

Researched, Written,
& Photographed by:

John Derrick
Natasha Derrick

Discover Paradise...

Hawaiian Style Organization LLC
www.HawaiianStyle.org

KAUA'I - MILE BY MILE GUIDE
The Best of the Garden Isle; First Edition

Published by:
Hawaiian Style Organization LLC
PO BOX 965
Columbia, South Carolina 29202-0965
www.HawaiianStyle.org

Published 2006
ISBN-13: 978-09773880-4-2
ISBN-10: 0-9773880-4-2
Library of Congress Control Number: 2006920400
Printed in the United States

Language Note: Hawai'i's two official languages are Hawaiian and English, the only state in the US with two official languages. In this guide we have attempted to use both the English and Hawaiian names of places when possible. There are only 13 letters in the Hawaiian alphabet: A, E, H, I K, L, M, N, O, P, U, W and the 'okina ('). The okina is a glottal stop like the sound between the ohs in "oh-oh" and is considered a consonant. In order to clarify pronunciation, you will often see the glottal stop (') or 'okina used on words in this guide such as Hawai'i. Due to printing restrictions, we will not use the macron, which is found above stressed vowels in the Hawaiian language. See page 220 for a 'crash course' of the Hawaiian language, including pronunciation.

All photographs (except satellite imagery and where otherwise noted) taken by John and Natasha Derrick. Satellite imagery courtesy of NASA.

Dedication

To our families and friends, who without their support and encouragement this book would not have been possible. Our greatest mahalos to them all.

Acknowledgements

For their encouragement, support, advice, and countless hours of proofreading our manuscripts: our parents, Dot & Charles Derrick, our good friends Alistair MacMillan, JoAnn Kosowan, and Loris Arthurton.

To David Hale for his immeasurable help and advice on photo equipment and photography for our books.

To all of those who sent useful information to us during the process of writing our book and those who asked questions along the way that helped us critique our work even more.

We send much gratitude to those who have read our book and given us feedback on the content, criticisms and compliments alike. Until we became authors we did not truly realize the importance of reader input and feedback.

To the county of Kaua'i and state of Hawai'i for providing and maintaining such a wonderful and diverse array of state parks and grounds to visit. To the park rangers who have always been helpful when navigating the trails of Koke'e State Park.

Finally, our sincerest appreciation to the citizens of Kaua'i for their selflessness in sharing their beautiful home with us all and for always surrounding us with aloha.

Mahalo nui loa to you all.

TABLE OF CONTENTS

Kaua'i Introduction

Aloha to the...
Garden Isle of Hawai'i

Kaua'i Basics

Starting with...
Planning & Itineraries

East Kaua'i

Starting in...
North Lihue

North Shore Kaua'i

Starting at...
Na 'Aina Kai Garden

South Kaua'i

Starting in...
West Lihue

West Kaua'i

Starting at...
Russian Fort Elisabeth

Kaua'i Conclusion

Ending with...
A Hui Hou

Aloha kakou to the

Garden Isle

INTRODUCTION

Kaua'i is an island full of splendor, raw beauty, culture, aloha, and ancient lore. Visiting the island of Kaua'i is like a journey back in time, back to the beginning of the main Hawaiian chain. Kaua'i is dubbed the "Garden Isle" for 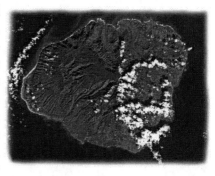 good reason, it is by far the 'greenest' of the islands and thus the most lush in all of Hawai'i. This jungle-like island can attribute its climate to the trade winds that blow over the land allowing the ancient volcanic peaks to catch rain from the sky and pull it down to the earth below. Mount Wai'ale'ale is one of these peaks and is the wettest spot on earth, averaging near 450-470 inches of rain a year. In 1985 a record setting 665.5 inches fell – that's 55 feet of rain! In fact, all that rain allows Kaua'i to be the only island in Hawai'i to have navigable rivers. Let that sink in... kayaking, canoeing, swimming, boating, and even jet skiing - in Hawai'i!

OK, so the rivers are interesting, the wettest spot sounds neat, but the rain still sounds like a downer, right? Well, don't let the rain scare you off just yet. Like on the other Hawaiian islands, the rain showers are usually brief and limited in their geographic size. It could be raining in one area, and five miles down the road it might be sunny and warm. Most showers are at night or in the early mornings and are usually inland in the mountainous areas. Plus, remember, no rain, no rainbows, and on Kaua'i rainbows are to die for. Have you ever seen a full double or triple rainbow? If you need a better reason than that, well, Kaua'i may be the wettest island in all Hawai'i, but it is also arguably the most beautiful island in the Hawaiian chain, if not quite possibly the whole world. The raw beauty and natural landscapes carved and etched into the isle through time make it a destination like no other. Some might say Kaua'i is as close to a masterpiece of creation as you'll ever find. From the lush valleys of the Na Pali coast to the deep and arid canyons of Waimea, Kaua'i is sure to please, delight, and amaze you like no other Hawaiian island can. After visiting Kaua'i, you may never view the rest of the world the same way again. Even the locals from the other Hawaiian islands come to vacation on Kaua'i – it's that good.

A double rainbow greets early risers over the city of Kapa'a on Kaua'i's coconut coast.

OVERVIEW OF KAUA'I, HAWAII

Kaua'i is the fourth largest landmass in the Hawaiian island chain that includes eight major islands and 124 islets. The archipelago consists of numerous volcanic islands in the central Pacific Ocean stretching in a 1,500-mile crescent from Kure Island in the northwest to the Big Island of Hawai'i in the east, encompassing an area of 6,459 square miles. The eight major islands at the eastern end of the chain are, from west to east, Niihau, Kaua'i, Oahu, Molokai, Lanai, Kahoolawe, Maui, and the Big Island of Hawai'i.

Our journey begins on the island of Kaua'i. Kaua'i is the oldest of all the main Hawaiian Islands, dating back some 5.1 million years. Kaua'i lies approximately 105 miles across the Kaua'i Channel, northwest of Oahu. The island is nearly circular in shape with a land area encompassing 533 square miles, that is 25 miles long by 33 miles wide at its furthest

K^{INTRODUCTION}AUAI

Few places on the earth can rival the island of Kaua'i's natural splendor and elegance. Over the last five million years, Kaua'i has transformed itself into a mecca of everything beautiful and pristine.

points. Of volcanic origin, the highest peaks on this mountainous island are Kawaikini, at 5,243 feet, followed by Mount Wai'ale'ale near the center of the island, at 5,148 feet above sea level. The wettest spot on earth, with an annual average rainfall of 450-470 inches, is located on the east side of Mount Wai'ale'ale. This high annual rainfall has eroded deep valleys in the central mountain, carving out ridges, canyons, and valleys with many scenic waterfalls.

Today, there is no known meaning behind the name of Kaua'i, but native tradition suggests the island was named after the son of the navigator who discovered the Hawaiian Islands.

The city of Lihue, on the island's southeast coast, is the seat of Kaua'i County and the largest city on the island. Waimea, on the island's southwest side and once the capital of Kaua'i, was the first place visited by explorer Captain James Cook in 1778. Waimea Town is located at the mouth of the Waimea River, whose flow formed one of the most scenic canyons in the world, 3000 foot deep Waimea Canyon. Mark Twain once dubbed it the "Grand Canyon of the Pacific."

Kaua'i is also home to the U.S. Navy's Pacific Missile Range Facility. It's tucked away in the canyons near Waimea, and unless you go looking for it, you'll never even know it is there.

The island of Kaua'i has also been a hot spot for feature films. Dozens of filmmakers and producers have chosen the Garden Isle for a backdrop in their movies. To name a few - *Lilo and Stitch, Jurassic Park, Indiana Jones, Dragonfly, Mighty Joe Young, Outbreak, Six Days Seven Nights, The Thorn Birds*, and *Hook*. If you remember the majestic green cliffs and lush jungle scenery from these movies – well, that's Kaua'i.

Kaua'i really is a true hidden gem of sorts. Over 90% of the island cannot be reached by road. In fact, the most beautiful part of the whole island has no road near it – and we like it that way. Kaua'i has roads stretching around it from the northwest coast, starting at Ke'e Beach, moving clockwise along the eastern coast (through Kapa'a and Lihue) and then around to the west coast (through Hanapepe and Waimea). Finally, it heads north up to the ridges of Waimea and Koke'e State Park overlooking the inaccessible Na Pali coast on the west side of the island. There is no way to drive from Waimea/Koke'e to the starting point, and there likely never will be (you'll have to turn around). The Alaka'i Swamp has stumped the U.S. Corps of Engineers on more than one occasion. The army's telephone poles from the last world war are all that remain of any attempt to navigate that part of the island. But don't worry, you can still see many of the wonders of Kaua'i by doing a bit of hiking. In our guide, we'll take you on a few of our favorite trails.

KAUAI
INTRODUCTION

SYNOPSIS OF OUR GUIDE

Our guidebook is designed to help you plan your vacation by providing in-depth information on the best of Kaua'i's places, beaches, hikes, and activities. And since our details are precise, down to the mile, and our ratings based on good instinct and experience, you can decide for yourself in good conscience which stops are right for you long before your own journey. We know your time on Kaua'i is precious, and we understand you don't want to waste your time on certain spots or activities. So we'll always be completely straightforward with you on our thoughts about each spot. Ultimately, you're the travel planner for your visit to Kaua'i, and hopefully by using our guide you too can have a wonderful experience in paradise.

In our guide, we'll be starting from the county seat of Kaua'i, Lihue, which is located on the eastern side of the island (see the map on page 18-19 for reference). From this point, we will first take you along Highway 56 heading north to Highway 560 before ending at the furthest point you can access via road on the northwest coast, Ke'e Beach. Then we'll restart at Lihue and travel clockwise along various highways until we end in Koke'e State Park at the Pu'u o Kila Lookout over the Kalalau Valley. We'll also mark trail locations from where they begin (i.e. Kalalau Trail extends 12 miles along Kaua'i's west coast, but since it starts at Ke'e Beach on the north shore, we'll list it at that location).

Lihue is the most logical starting point for our guide because all mile markers will count up, which makes referencing and finding spots much easier. You can always view our maps for verification of stops as well. You'll probably see quickly that many spots are clumped together on Kauaʻi, and that the northern coastline of Kauaʻi is, by far, the most popular part of the island. All in all our entire guide should detail about a week's worth of stops, sightseeing, and hiking. We have included a small section on planning and itineraries that may help you prepare accordingly (page 33). We'll attempt to note time estimates to the best of our ability, and as always we'll include our rankings. This should help you determine which spots to visit in relation to the days you have available to sightsee.

Our guidebook is structured to help you easily find the places you are looking for without tediously flipping through the pages. Our index and clear table of contents should make finding any particular spot a breeze. For travelers looking for the very best of activities, those that rank above the run of the mill, we have developed a "Top 5" section for the best places, beaches, hikes, waterfalls, and activities (page 73). Our guidebook also utilizes a number of features you won't find in most other guidebooks including our numerous photos, ratings, detailed maps, time estimates, frequent updates, and our mile by mile directions. Here's a bit more about what we will present you with in our guide:

• *Photographs:* Our guide attempts to include a photograph of every major stop we write about. In fact, we include so many photographs we can even use the term "fully-illustrated" on our cover. Plus, there are no tricks or fancy camera work with our guide's photos. The main difference between our photos and what you might see are the weather factors and/or seasonal changes (i.e. - waterfall flow rates). No other guide on the market contains as many photos.

K*INTRODUCTION*I
KAUAI

• *Place Ratings:* Each spot has a rating (1-5; 5 best). None of our ratings have been influenced by anyone or anything other than what you will see/experience at each spot. If we liked the place, we'll tell you we liked it, and if we didn't, you're going to know about that too. Candor is better than embellishment in our opinion; so you'll know what to expect at each spot. Here's a look at the ratings we use throughout our guide:

☆☆☆☆☆ - Avoid   ★★★☆☆ - Good

★☆☆☆☆ - Poor   ★★★★☆ - Excellent

★★☆☆☆ - So-So   ★★★★★ - Must See

• *Detailed Maps:* Maps... you love them or you hate them, but we've worked hard to make sure our maps are simple, yet clear and precise. All our maps contain mile markers, general spot locations, cities, and major roads. We keep our maps simple because some maps are just plain too busy. You need some huge key explaining all the symbols just so you can decode them. Who wants to do that on their vacation? We keep it clean, clear, and simple.

• *Time Estimates:* When applicable, we'll clue you in to just how long we think you can expect to spend at each location. We are especially fond of including estimates on hikes, as there is nothing worse than underestimating the time you need for a long hike. Flashlight hiking isn't something we'd like to get anyone into.

• *Frequent Updates:* Life is constantly changing. The same goes for guidebooks, even those on slow-paced Kauai. We make it a point to provide any updates or changes to the information in this guidebook available on our web site 24/7:

www.HawaiianStyle.org

• *Mile markers:* Mile markers on Kaua'i are pretty reliable and we use that to our advantage. Our guide gives directions based on mile markers around the island of Kaua'i so that you can locate and view each stop easily and enjoyably.

Waimea Canyon in west Kaua'i.

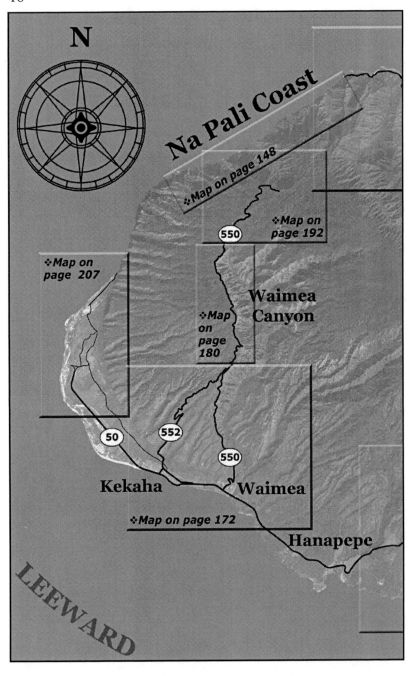

N

Na Pali Coast

❖Map on page 148

550

❖Map on page 192

❖Map on page 207

Waimea Canyon

❖Map on page 180

50

552

550

Kekaha

Waimea

❖Map on page 172

Hanapepe

LEEWARD

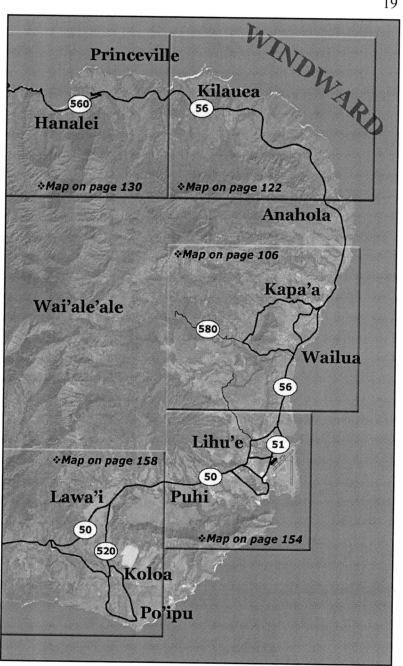

Princeville

560

Hanalei

Kilauea

56

❖*Map on page 130*

❖*Map on page 122*

WINDWARD

Anahola

❖*Map on page 106*

Wai'ale'ale

Kapa'a

580

Wailua

56

Lihu'e

51

❖*Map on page 158*

50

Lawa'i

Puhi

50

❖*Map on page 154*

520

Koloa

Po'ipu

K*INTRODUCTION*T AUAI

KAUA'I BY REGION

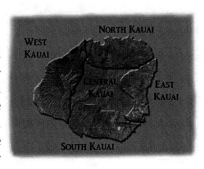

Dividing Kaua'i up based on geography is practically impossible. The island is round and very diverse from one area to the next. For that reason, we've divided the island by standard regions: North, South, East, West, keeping it simple, Kaua'i style. There is also an inaccessible Central region which we will discuss momentarily.

Kaua'i has a relatively small population in relation to the other islands in the chain. It is the fourth largest island in area but only has a population of near 57,000, pretty small by most standards. Like most of the other Hawaiian Islands, and perhaps more so, Kaua'i changes very quickly geographically, including weather conditions. As we have already noted, only about 10% of Kaua'i is drivable. From the starting point of our guide at Ke'e Beach (sea level on the north shore) to the end point at Koke'e State Park (4000 feet above sea level on the north west shore), the straight drive can easily take 2-3 hours. Plus, the speed limits on Kaua'i are low, and the island is infamous for this fact, so don't expect to get anywhere in a hurry on Kaua'i. Many might say that's the point, but most folks live in an entirely different world than you'll find on Kaua'i. Be sure to remember that things are much more laid back and time is relative here to that pace of life. That said, let's take a look at the regions of Kaua'i.

• East Kaua'i

There are many people who
will call East Kaua'i the
Coconut Coast, and once
you visit you'll see why.
For miles along the shoreline there are hundreds of
coconut trees. East Kaua'i

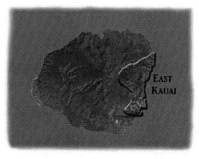

will also be where rain chances increase as the trade winds
blow in from the Pacific. The average rainfall varies along the
coastline, but you can expect to see a little more than on the
south and west sides - between 45 and 60 inches a year. Head
mauka (inland) towards Wai'ale'ale or Kawaikini, though,
rain increases by the foot, literally. The average temperature
is much cooler in this region than the south or west at around
70 ºF.

*The premier attraction in east Kaua'i is the popular double-tiered
Wailua Falls. We won't argue that!*

K*INTRODUCTION*I
KAUAI

The east coast is probably the second most popular part of the island, and most of the resorts are along this stretch, especially in Kapa'a and Lihue. Plus, there are plenty of attractions gracing the region, from Wailua and Opaeka'a Falls to the Fern Grotto, all near the Wailua River.

Lihue is where you begin your journey on Kaua'i, as it is where the airport and county seat are located. You'll also find the Kaua'i Museum there, along with Kalapaki Beach. If you head north from Lihue, you'll pass through the popular resort area of Kapa'a. It is a small oceanfront town that's getting ever so close to the North Shore. It is also right on the edge of Wailua River State Park and Lydgate Beach Park.

Other towns you'll find on the east side include Wailua, Hanamaulu, and Anahola.

The hidden gem of east Kaua'i is definitely the "blue hole" located inside the crater of Wai'ale'ale. From this vantage point you can view the famous "wall of tears."

• *North Shore Kaua'i*

NORTH KAUAI

As on all the Hawaiian Islands, this region is typically known as the famous "North Shore." The North Shore has a mild average temperature in the mid to low 70's, but much of it receives a lot more rain - up to 120 inches a year in some places. This makes it green, lush, and very tropical. As we mentioned earlier though, don't let the rain spoil your plans. It might be raining in one spot and sunny a mile or two up the road – plus, most of the rain falls at night. Rain gear isn't a bad idea, but don't let the showers rain on your parade.

For all those looking to relax after exploring the wild western coast of Kaua'i, let North Kaua'i be the spot to indulge yourself in all things less-complicated and more laid-back. Ha'ena Beach Park (seen above) is just one of many delightful places to kick back and relax.

KAUA I
INTRODUCTION

The Hanalei Lookout offers a stunning view of the Hanalei Valley and the numerous taro fields planted there. Taro is used by Hawaiians to make an edible purple paste called poi.

One of the most popular resort areas is also located on the north shore of Kaua'i, Princeville. Princeville is a large and popular resort area overlooking the cliffs of Hanalei and Hanalei Bay with everything you could ever need to make the perfect vacation. Just hold onto your wallet, things can be pricey here. Houses in this area go for too much money and way too much money. Compared to the west coast of Kaua'i, this is Beverly Hills.

Other towns you'll find on the south side include Kilauea, Ha'ena, and Hanalei with it's beautiful bay and beaches.

• *South Kaua'i*

The southern side of Kaua'i is hot, dry, and arid averaging about 35-40 inches of rain a year. The average temperature is 78 °F, but don't be surprised if temps get into the high 80's or even

SOUTH KAUAI

90's in this region. Though far from the popular North Shore and scarcely populated, the South side has a lot to offer. The biggest attractions here are the perfect beaches around the Poipu area and Spouting Horn (seen below).

The Poipu area stretches around Makahuena Point and is a popular tourist destination, filled with hotels, condos, resorts, shopping, and vacation rentals.

Other towns you'll find on the south side include Kalaheo, Koloa, Lawai, and Omao.

K**INTRODUCTION**I
KAUAI

• West Kaua'i

WEST
KAUAI

For the most part, West Kaua'i is impassable, filled with mountainous terrain and valleys that make roads impossible to build here. This side of Kaua'i is most famous for the Na Pali coast and the trails and hikes that stretch far and wide across it.

The western side of Kaua'i is so remarkably beautiful that you could spend the majority of your vacation exploring it. An overlook of the Kalalau Valley, as seen above from the Kalalau Lookout, is just one of the many beautiful places along the Na Pali coast that makes this part of Kaua'i such a rare gem.

West Kaua'i includes the Waimea town area, Waimea Canyon, and Polihale Beach State Park. The weather on this side of the island varies greatly. In the valleys of Na Pali, rain can come down in buckets at any given time as clouds fill in between the ridged valley walls. On average though, the weather at the coast and near Waimea Canyon is hot (75-80 °F) and dry with about 25 inches average rainfall a year. The Koke'e State Park area is a mix of wet and dry, with trails toward the Pali coast being drier than those heading inland. The Alaka'i Swamp trails are typically on the wetter side, so don't be surprised by the occasional storm. The swampy conditions are also due to the rainfall that occurs on the mountains to the east of the swamp and then flows down into this area of Kaua'i.

The west is pretty remote in comparison to the rest of the island. It's usually sunny when you're not heading mauka (inland) and dry most days of the year on the coast. The town of Waimea leaves a lot to be desired for most visitors, but to the people that call it home, it's, well, home. The road from Waimea heading towards Polihale will leave you wondering what continent you're on. It turns to dusty desert in this area. The Barking Sands Pacific Missile Range is also located on the west coast of Kaua'i. This is a naval base out in the middle of nowhere on an incredibly long and vacant beach. From near Polihale you can see where they've bored into the ancient cliffs to store military supplies – and we're just fine with not knowing what.

Other towns you'll find on the west side include Eleele, Hanapepe, Kamakani, Port Allen, Kapaka, and Mana.

K̄AUAI

• *Central Kaua'i*

By now you've likely come to realize that Kaua'i is an island that dares to be discovered but is not always easily revealed. At the same time you've likely come to appreciate  the meaning of words like "hidden gem" and "natural treasure," as Kaua'i is certainly full of both. All four of Kaua'i's main regions can be easily accessed by the primary road encircling the island. At least all those places are "pretty easy" to reach compared to accessing central Kaua'i. With no roads heading into the middle of the island, your only chances to see this mystical part of the island are by air or by foot.

For those daring enough to visit Wai'ale'ale on the east, then you'll already have a taste of what central Kaua'i has to offer. In reality, the "blue hole" of Wai'ale'ale is in central Kaua'i, but the only way to access it is via a road in east Kaua'i, thus we classify it there. But "blue hole" is as far into central Kaua'i as you'll venture by vehicle, and even then you'd better expect to hike a bit to get the best views into the crater.

Central Kaua'i is the untouched, undeveloped, and all-to-often unseen part of the garden isle. So if you're looking to discover this part of Kaua'i, plan ahead and book a helicopter tour because it really is your best option.

THE FORBIDDEN ISLAND OF NI'IHAU

When you come to Kaua'i you can't help but notice the small island on the horizon as you near the west coast. This is the forbidden island of Ni'ihau, the smallest of the inhabited islands, measuring about 16 miles by 14 miles. Visitation is not allowed on Ni'ihau, and the islands 250 inhabitants are all pure-blooded Hawaiians who live in a place as close to traditional Hawai'i as you will ever find.

Hawaiian legend states that Ni'ihau is the original home of the volcano goddess, Pele. Today she lives and breaths her fire on the Big Island of Hawai'i at the far eastern end of the chain. The climate of Ni'ihau is dry and often quite arid, there are no mountains stretching into the clouds to pull the rain down onto the land below. Ironically, the largest lake in Hawai'i can be found on the island, but it is often shallow and muddy.

KAUAI

Ni'ihau is privately owned by the Robinson family of Kaua'i, and it has been in their family since 1864 when it was purchased with the hope of raising cattle on it. The Robinsons are the descendents of the Sinclair family, who originally purchased the island from King Kamehameha V. It was in 1863 that the Scottish-born Eliza Sinclair set out to find a place to settle and raise their cattle. After turning down land on Oahu, they planned to head to California and make their purchase there, but Kamehameha offered to sell them the remote island of Ni'ihau 17 miles off the coast of Kaua'i. As the Sinclairs toured the island, they found a lush green island flourishing with all they could hope for. This would be the place they would buy. They made the purchase for a negotiated $10,000 and the island was theirs, sort of. At first many of the residents of Ni'ihau refused to acknowledge them as the owners, including some who had deeds from Kamehameha III stating their ownership to various pieces of the island. Negotiations took place and in the end the Sinclairs paid a tenth of what they had originally paid for the whole island to obtain the land, a mere 50 acres. It was years later the Sinclairs learned the truth about Ni'ihau, that it was no green oasis or flourishing island with the ability to sustain cattle. In the year of their purchase Ni'ihau had experienced a rare rainy spell, causing the island to burst into bloom. In their dismay they purchased a 21,000 acre parcel of land on Kaua'i for their range plans and later expanded that amount to 51,000 acres, all of which they own to this very day, only now as the Robinson family. They still live on their estate on the island of Kaua'i.

Today, Ni'ihau's residents continue to live with no phone service and limited electricity. The locals work on the Robinsons' ranching and farming operations. Food to the island is provided by import from Kaua'i. The journey to and from is quite primitive by today's standards. It's performed in old military transport boats. Not surprisingly the primary language of the island is Hawaiian, and many native Hawaiians still come to the island to study and learn the language. Of course residents are free to come and go as they please, so Ni'ihau continues to exert an influence on modern Hawaiian culture far beyond its size. Many of the children on the island will even leave for higher education purposes, sometimes returning to their home and sometimes not.

In recent years, the Robinson family has allowed limited access via helicopter to outsiders wishing to visit unpopulated portions of the island, and there are indications that their financial situation may cause further loosening of the restrictions on visitors. The Robinsons have also now begun a number of tourism programs on their Kaua'i land near Waimea canyon, as well as developed plans for a new resort in west Kaua'i.

Today there are many grave concerns among native Hawaiians throughout Hawai'i about the future of Ni'ihau and what will happen to it if the Robinson family is no longer able to maintain their stewardship of the island. Taxes have created a burden on the family that leaves their ownership in question in the near future. Even those who resent the Robinsons' ownership of the island realize and agree on the importance of the Robinsons maintaining that control and ownership that has allowed the Ni'ihau tradition to continue uninterrupted.

Though few of us will ever step on the shores of the forbidden island, we can still take a piece of it back home with us. Ni'ihau Shell leis have long been treasured for their beauty and painstaking craftsmanship. The long process of making a necklace begins with collecting the tiny shells from ocean swept beaches and grading them according to color and size. When you consider that a dozen shells would fit on your thumbnail, and the most prized are as small as the letter "a" on this page, you can begin to appreciate the difficulty of the task. The necklace may be strung in a variety of ways. We have been told stories of how the women of Ni'ihau will spend hours upon hours, days upon days looking for the shells to make a single necklace. Their price is high, but they are a true Hawaiian treasure to be had. They are a representation of the island that remains kapu (off limits) to the outside world and of tradition that dates back as far as the inhabitation of the islands themselves. True Hawai'i is still alive in the heart of Ni'ihau and hopefully will continue to be for future generations.

Ni'ihau as seen from Polihale Beach on west Kaua'i.

KAUA'I TRAVEL PLANNING

Before you pack your bags, put on your Aloha shirt, and jump the Pacific Ocean to head to Kaua'i, there are a few basic things you should know about the island, its people, weather, geography, and lifestyle. Furthermore, this section of our guide is meant to help you plan the perfect Kaua'i vacation by covering some of the most essential facts all visitors need to know. On the following pages we'll cover some of these facts and planning tips including money, when to visit, the weather, what you'll need to pack, the best way to get to the island, online trip planning, accommodations and car rental tips, and conclude with itineraries for the one and two week travelers in the following section of our guide.

• *Money*

As a traveler to Hawai'i you will likely come under one of two conditions, the budget traveler or the traveler looking to live the high life. Believe it or not, Hawai'i may be just about the only place you can choose one style over another and leave with the same experience. Most people who have tried both lifestyles have reported having just as good a time either way. So whether you conscientiously save money in Hawai'i by seeking out great deals or alternatively spend loads of money on resorts, tours, and fine dining, you'll likely leave with the same great experience. That's the magic of Hawai'i - the real gift is what's around you, the natural beauty of the island, the people, and the friendly atmosphere. Sure you can buy great things, participate in amazing activities, and eat in first class restaurants while here, and we certainly encourage travelers to live life in Hawai'i to the max. On the same token, we also encourage everyone to enjoy the best part of Hawai'i, the part that's free to everyone... the spirit of Aloha. Ultimately, our point is you don't have to spend a fortune on Kaua'i to have a good time. Our book is primarily designed for those on a budget who want to get away from their hotels and condos to see the great outdoors, participate in fun activities that won't break the bank, and experience life on Hawai'i like a local would.

Our last suggestion regarding money is to pay for most of your bills and purchases in Hawai'i with credit, debit, or check. Traveling with cash, even in Hawai'i, is usually never a good idea. There are countless stories told about folks who have lost their money and thus lost their fun. On just our last trip around the island we ran into one poor soul who had lost his wallet containing all his money on a beach. You can cancel checks and plastic cards, but you can't replace your cash. This isn't to say you shouldn't bring any cash, but as a general rule of thumb we would suggest purchasing most things with an alternative payment form.

• *When to Visit*

A really popular question we hear is "When should I come to Kaua'i?" This question is typically followed by "What's the weather like at that time?" You can learn about the general weather conditions in our weather section starting on page 38. Here we'll discuss our favorite times of the year to visit and why.

Spring: The beginning of the "dry season" on most of the islands, this is one of the most ideal times to visit. The weather is almost always perfect and in general this is the best time to find good travel bargains. After mid-April most airfare and lodging prices drop as a result of "high season" ending. The last week of April and first week of May are often a time when the most Japanese visitors will arrive due to the "Golden Week" holiday in Japan. Water temperatures measure near the high 70-degree mark this time of year, and the surf begins to die down some as the trade winds let up. The best part of the spring is the fresh flowers, fruit, and vegetation that can be seen around the island. The spring is our favorite time to visit.

Summer: Typically summer is classified on Hawai'i as the "low season." We're not exactly sure why as it seems to us this is when the most families visit the island, mainly due to children being out of school. The same rule applies for local children on the island. This is their summer and they often frequent the same beaches, trails, and places you'll be visiting too. The summer months are always the warmest on the island, and temperatures can reach as high as the 90's under the right conditions. Combined with the high humidity, the heat can occasionally be unpleasant for some travelers not accustomed to it. Surf is at its lowest during the summer, and the rain clouds are few and far between except on the windward coast. Water temperatures usually rise above the 80-degree mark. While a rare event, the summer months are also hurricane season in Hawai'i, and the last major storm to hit Hawai'i was Iniki in September 1992, when it came ashore Kaua'i as a strong category 3 (border-line category 4) storm. In our opinion, the summer is simply too warm for a lot of outdoor hiking and adventure. The prices are nice on the wallet, but the sun combined with the humidity can make going anywhere but the beach a chore. We'd say come a few months earlier in the spring or a few months later in the fall if given a choice.

Fall: The "rainy season" begins in November, and there are days where rain showers will dominate on the windward coast. In recent years, however, even the rainy season has been pretty dry. "High season" for traveling begins in mid-December which typically causes rates for flights, tours, and accommodations to rise. In general the fall months and the spring months are very similar.

Winter: By the time winter is in full swing, the "high season" has begun on the islands. The high temperature remains a comfortable average of near 78 degrees. Water temperatures are often around 74 degrees during this period, and swimming can be rough as a result of the higher surf. If you're coming to Hawai'i to see any surfing events, then this is definitely the time to come. The north shore of Kaua'i attracts countless surfing enthusiasts during this time of the year. In our opinion, winter is usually the least desirable time to visit the island. Despite the waterfalls usually being more active due to the rain, the combination of higher prices, wetter weather in general, and cooler temperatures has never sat well with us when you can easily visit during the spring or fall for much cheaper prices and better weather.

In general that should help you decide which season is best for your visit. We personally prefer the spring but some visitors are equally partial to the winter and would always recommend it above any other time. Regardless of what time you visit, we believe you are bound to have a good time. Consider what it is you are looking to do on the island and make your decision from there.

Our next topic covers the other popular question, weather and what to expect while visiting the island.

A visit during the spring months can be most rewarding, as the Plumeria are in full bloom, and the light trade winds carry the scent of fresh flowers all over the island.

KPLANNINGAUAI

• *Weather Conditions*

While it's always going to be close to impossible to predict the weather months or even weeks ahead of your vacation, you can look at past weather and climatic variables to determine what is likely to occur. Below we'll go over some of the most common concerns about Kaua'i weather. If nothing else, you'll have a general idea of what to expect. As always, be sure to check local weather through the TV stations during your stay for day to day updates.

Kaua'i's General Weather Patterns: The best thing about Kaua'i's weather is that it is very localized. You may be driving along the island and be in a rain storm one minute and in bright sun the next. This variety of weather allows you to fully experience Kaua'i and its sun-drenched beaches, misty rainbow-filled valleys, pristine waterfalls, cool highlands, and lush mountains.

One mistake a lot of people make when they visit Hawai'i is assuming there is a wet and/or dry season like back home, not so here on Kaua'i. Granted there are two distinct times of year and weather patterns due to the trade winds, but there is no defined "rainy season." On average, the summer months are the driest and sunniest, but they are also the most humid and warmest. The winter months usually bring more rain to the windward side of the island, north and east, but prolonged rain storms are uncommon. The south shore is the driest part of the island year round. Also, consider that Kaua'i is dubbed the "Garden Isle" for a reason, and that rain does often pop up on the island helping it keep its lush green appearance. In our opinion, the best parts of the island are mostly on the windward side, so keeping a small poncho with you during hikes or other outdoor activities might be a good idea. Unless you hike into any valleys, where clouds can build up and stick around a while, you're likely only to experience rain in short spells.

Kaua'i Temperatures: Kaua'i is fortunate in that it has a mild and pleasant temperature throughout the year, the largest complaint likely being the humidity for those not used to it. There is hardly any difference between night and day temperatures year round. The occasional storm or the trades winds are the exception to the rule, but even then temperatures don't vary by much. The average high and low in the summer is around 85 and 71 respectively, while the average high and low in the winter is 78 and 62 respectively.

The temperature estimates only apply near sea level, please keep in mind that elevation changes will alter the temperatures. With every 1,000 foot climb in elevation, the temperature, on average, drops another 3.5 degrees. The highest point accessible by road on Kaua'i is around 4,000 feet, so that averages out to about a 15 degree drop in temperature from what it was at sea level. In the winter months a jacket or light sweater can be helpful, especially in the chilliest parts of the morning around sunrise.

If it's the ocean temperatures you're wondering about, rest assured you'll find warm temperatures year round. Ocean temperatures remain pretty comfortable through-out the year ranging from 80 degrees in the summer to a milder 74 in the winter.

K<small>PLANNING</small>I
K A U A I

• *What to pack*

Regardless of how much you've traveled in the past and where you've been there is one good rule to follow when coming to Hawai'i, leave as much as you can at home. Seriously, bring only what you'll need during your stay and nothing more. For starters, schlepping around three suitcases is NOT what you want to be doing after getting off a long plane ride. Next, consider that long pants, dress clothes, and anything else formal really has no use in Hawai'i (unless you are staying in a very exclusive resort). Kaua'i is one of the most casual islands in the chain, and there might be one restaurant on the whole island that requires a tie. Chances are a pair of shorts and an old Aloha shirt are all you'll need for even some fine dining.

As far as clothing goes, that's usually a few pairs of shorts, several T-shirts, sandals or flip-flops, and a good visor or hat, anything made of a cotton blend is usually good. A light jacket might also be nice for those visits to higher elevations around Waimea Canyon. Don't bring your winter coat to Kaua'i. Even during the winter it rarely gets "cold" here like it does on Maui's Haleakala or the Big Island's Mauna Kea. The absolute highest point you'll reach by road is just over 4,000 feet on the island, and as noted in the weather section, that's on average a 15-degree drop in temperature from the conditions at sea-level. Temperatures below 50 are pretty rare at even the highest elevations on Kaua'i.

With the motto, "less is more" in mind, here are a few other items to bring. Sunblock (the UV on Hawai'i is typically 10+ in the spring, summer, and fall), a backpack (for any hikes) and a water bottle, slippers (flip flops, show-

Make sure you leave your worries behind when you visit. Otherwise you might risk losing them to a vibrant Kaua'i sunset forever.

er shoes, zoris), mask, snorkel, and fins (or rent locally instead), two bathing suits (one to wear while the other dries) and a cover-up, camera and film (or digital cards), lightweight raincoat or poncho (for mountain/rain forest hiking), bug spray with DEET (for any forest hikes), flashlight (if the sun goes down before your hike ends or for night walks on the beach), hiking boots and hiking rods, and most importantly a list of all your troubles to leave behind.

K PLANNING I
KAUAI

• *How to get here*

For the most part your options are pretty limited on how you get to Kaua'i. You can come by boat or by air, and that's just about it. Either method of transportation is fine, but we personally prefer to arrive by air. A long cruise can "spoil" the joys of arriving on Hawai'i's shores by simply taking too long. There is something to be said about that built up anticipation of just waiting to step foot on the island. That's why we recommend flying as the best travel method. You can leave home and arrive in paradise on the same day, and even for travelers on the far east coast

Remember, rising with the sun each day will get you far ahead of the crowds and any traffic that might occur in Kaua'i (and it does often in East Kaua'i). As a general rule, hardly anyone likes to get up very early on their vacation to paradise, but if you do it, you'll likely be glad you did. For US mainland travelers, use the time change to your advantage. The photo above is of Ke'e Beach at sunset, proving the setting sun is equally worth staying up for in the evening.

of the mainland, it's only a 12 hour flight. OK, so that's not exactly a short flight, but it beats coming by boat. Besides, that plane ride gives you a chance to peruse your travel books and plans and refresh your memory before you arrive. Just don't expect to jump off the plane and start "doing it all" after you arrive. That said, for some of you this next paragraph is going to be redundant and obvious, but for others it will be good information to have.

Perhaps you've flown on long trips before and perhaps you haven't. We're going to assume most folks have likely never flown on a flight over 5-7 hours before and we're also going to assume that most visitors utilizing our guide are from the mainland United States. If you're traveling from even further east, like Europe, then you'll need to adjust our advice as needed to accommodate you. If you're traveling from the west, like Australia, then take our advice in reverse. When traveling from the west your jet-lag will be worse coming than going. But most visitors are coming from the east, and whether you're coming from sunny California or chilly New York the shortest amount of time you'll be on a plane is about five to six hours. If you're flying from New York, Boston, or most any other town on the east coast you can expect to add another four to five hours to that number. In general, planes will have to fly into headwinds on their way west towards the islands, and thus you will notice your flight to the islands taking longer than your trip back home from the islands. Most visitors will also have to first make a stop in Honolulu, as there are few flights that fly directly into Lihue airport. Regardless of how long it takes you to arrive, the fact of the matter is you likely will experience some jet lag arriving, even from the east, so take it easy that first day and get some rest. Depending on when you visit you'll gain between two to six hours (Hawai'i does not observe daylight saving time) if coming from the US mainland. Our advice to travelers is always the same, attempt to keep your schedule close to what you had back home. Other guidebooks will tell you to covert yourself to Hawai'i time as soon as possible, but we won't. Here's why:

If you're coming from the east coast in the spring, as an example, you're going to gain six hours during your flight. So if you leave at 6am and arrive at 4pm, you've actually been awake a lot longer than it sounds. Back home it's actually 10pm when you arrive in Hawai'i, so you've already had a full day. We believe that by keeping to your regular schedule you can avoid the worst cases of jet lag, plus you'll have a leg up on most other travelers. If you can continue to get to bed early after sunset in Hawai'i, say around 8-10pm Hawai'i time, then you can get up a lot earlier than most visitors and hit the road far ahead of the crowds. For an east coast traveler, even a wake-up call of 5am in Hawai'i is the equivalent to 11am back home. It is our opinion you should use this to your advantage. When all is said and done it will also make your journey back home a lot easier too. Losing three to six hours heading home to the west is a lot harder than most people think.

Regardless of how you arrive in Kaua'i, make sure you pack light, prepare for your trip accordingly, and take it easy the first day you arrive. A good night's rest and a good meal after a long day's journey will refresh you for the rest of your vacation. Also, leave the fast-paced mainland behind you, relax to Kaua'i's lifestyle now.

• *Planning your trip online*

Whether you are a fan of the internet or not it is arguably one of the greatest tools available in the world today. Entire companies are built upon it, as was our own originally for over four years, and it has become a great asset for travel planners everywhere. Online travel companies like Expedia.com, Travelocity.com, Orbitz.com, etc offer travelers the chance to book every aspect of their vacation in the privacy and comfort of their own homes. Your flight, rental car, and accommodations can all be booked together to save you even more money. Plus, you can mix and match various combinations of flights and rooms to create the perfect deal for you. Our favorite online company to book through is Expedia. We've used them for countless trips and every time been pleased with their services. While a rarity to have to call and talk with customer support, even that was a pleasant experience, and we were helped courteously and quickly.

Expedia now also offers additional "activity packages" during your checkout, including the option to be greeted with a lei at Lihue airport. While always wise to compare prices, we have found that most of their "activity packages" are reasonably priced in comparison to other companies.

And speaking of activity packages and online companies, we have a recommendation there too. We have enjoyed booking several activities through a company named "Hawai'i Activities - Book It Hawai'i." This company gives you instant access to the largest selection of the best Hawai'i tours and activities, Hawai'i tourist attractions, sightseeing tours, and unique Hawaiian adventures. We have a special section set up on our web site for travelers utilizing our book:

www.hawaiianstyle.org/activities/kauai.php

If you're looking for more information on our favorite activities (some of which we anonymously booked online), see our "Top 5 Activities" section on page 94. The real point is that there are dozens and dozens of web sites available online that provide you with ways to book your perfect vacation to Kaua'i. We have listed our favorites above, as we have personal experience with them and have enjoyed their services.

We also have a few other free web sites which may aid you in planning your trip, including our free online travel help forum.

Planning: *www.HawaiianStyleTravel.com/KauaiGuide/*

Photos: *www.HawaiianStylePhotos.com/Kauai/*

Help Forum: *www.HawaiianStyleTravel.com/forum/*

• *Accommodations & Rental Tips*

On Kaua'i a rental car is definitely the best option for getting around the island and viewing all the sights we detail in our book. The rental rates in Hawai'i are some of the cheapest anywhere in the world because the competition is fierce.

There is no bus service on the island and taxi services are both expensive and illogical for sight-seeing purposes. Mopeds and bikes can be a practical alternative for day excursions along the drier south shore, but are not as useful in other parts of the island, especially where steep inclines prevail such as on Waimea Canyon Drive in west Kaua'i.

Car Rental Tips: Ultimately, your best bet is to get a rental for your stay. Below are some tips when acquiring your rental car:

1.) As previously stated in this guide, we recommend you book your rental online as many rental companies have online specials. Booking your rental together with a flight and/or accommodation will also save you money.

2.) Book as far in advance as possible. Depending on when you travel the rates may increase or decrease according to demand from other travelers.

3.) When possible, rent 2, 3, 5 day, or week long packages as these are generally priced lower than any other.

4.) When given the option to leave the rental office with a paid full tank of gas or having to fill it back up before you return it, take the first option. The rates that most

rental agencies charge per gallon are typically only pennies cheaper than the going rate on the island, but it's still a way to save some money. Otherwise, before you return the car you have to fill the car back up with gas yourself. If you don't, the rental company will charge you a much higher rate to refuel the car once back in their possession. If you plan to do a lot of driving, more than one tank of gas, then we definitely recommend you pay for the gas up front when you acquire your rental. That way you can return the car with as much or little gas as you have left in the car at that time without having to worry about refueling on the last day of your trip.

5.) As far as insurance goes, expect to hear the sales pitch telling you it's needed. We can almost hear the statistics now on Hawai'i roads and accident costs. Don't let the rental folks talk you into anything you don't need. Consider the following: The rental insurance they want to sell you is temporary insurance, but the fact is, you might very well already have it. Check with your insurance agent for your personal vehicles to see if you're covered. If you do already have rental insurance, you can save a bundle by avoiding this cost. Second, check with the credit card company you make the purchase with, as they may also provide you protection as a cardholder. Just be sure to clarify with your credit card company what they cover and what the limits are.

6.) Speaking of credit cards, expect to pay with one. Some companies may accept checks, but they definitely won't accept cash. Also don't just assume if you book ahead of time that you've paid all the fees associated with the rental. Occasionally additional fees will be charged at the time of the rental, one of which we detail next.

7.) The "under age" curse of renting in Hawai'i. This is one of the biggest and most despised surprises to all renters under the age of 25. In Hawai'i you are obligated by law to pay an "underage" fee for the risk the rental companies must take to insure you to drive on the island. This fee can be as much as $25 a day or more and quickly adds up. Also as far as we know, if you're under 21, you can't even rent a vehicle on Kaua'i.

8.) If your car breaks down while on Kaua'i be sure to call the 800 number provided with your rental package. If you fail to call them first in the event of an emergency, your expenses may not be covered.

9.) If you arrive and are told the model you reserved is not available, or isn't what you were looking for, you'll have the opportunity to "upgrade/downgrade" accordingly. This could be a bait and switch tactic, or they may just be overstocked on larger models, so be careful. If you're good at negotiating you might be able to get a larger vehicle at a really good rate, so don't feel shy about pressing them for the better vehicle at the same rate you already paid. After all, it's their fault for not having your model, not your's. Usually you'll be given the upgrade at the same rate, but if not, definitely argue it. If all else fails, cancel your rental with them and go to a competitor. If they actually let you walk away from the desk empty-handed you're probably better at another company anyway.

10.) Be prepared to wait once you arrive, the lines at most rental counters can be long and require patience.

Accommodation Tips: Unless you're planning to camp on the island, you're going to need a place to stay during your visit. Kaua'i, like most Hawaiian islands, has quite a variety of places to stay. Here are a few tips for selecting the perfect hotel, condo, resort, or house/cabin rental.

1.) As we've said already, booking online is your best bet for discovering good values and saving money. Booking a room along with a car or flight will especially save you money, as many online companies have pre-negotiated rates for "packaged" trips.

2.) Many guidebooks provide 20-30 pages of details on each and every hotel, condo, and resort on the island. In our opinion it's wasted space because most of that information is readily available on the internet. If you're following our advice of booking online, check to see if the company has a rating system set up for the "accommodations" segment of your booking. Most of the companies we've dealt with online do, including our favorite, Expedia. They even provide user comments from multiple travelers who have already stayed on the premises. Naturally, some companies will log on and attempt to skew their ratings, so we typically look for places with five or more ratings with in-depth comments. Any written review that both compliments and critiques the place is where you'll find your best advice. To date we haven't been steered wrong using this method, and we always try to follow up with our own rating after the fact. We encourage you to do the same. Ultimately, this system of reading multiple reviews by multiple travelers is better in our opinion than us giving you our two cents about our single experience with a place.

3.) Look for condos if you're in the "do-it-yourself" crowd. We consider our style of traveling as such, and thus we tend to lean towards condo rentals versus resorts or hotels. Our favorite thing about condos is the kitchen and fully-furnished rooms. Normally this gives visitors a

chance to do laundry in their room and reduce the clothing taken on their trip. Plus, the full kitchen is nice for fixing meals to take on the go during the day, especially if you're looking to save some money by preparing your own meals. Let's face it, you can't exactly pull up to a McDonald's while on a 10 mile hike. The kitchen allows you to store and prepare food for your daily excursions and this is a huge advantage in our opinion. Most resorts and/ or hotels (except the nicer ones) often do not have a refrigerator in the room. Condos aren't any more expensive than the alternatives, and can often be cheaper. Besides it may just feel more "homey" than a sterile resort room. When we come to Kaua'i we like to immerse ourselves in the full Hawaiian experience. The condo allows us to do that in a way no hotel or resort will.

Well there you go, the best basic tips we can offer for planning your own trip to the beautiful Garden Isle of Kaua'i. We sincerely hope that our tips and advice on planning your trip to Kaua'i have been useful and insightful. If you have any comments and/or additions you feel would fit in well here, we encourage you to contact us and let us know. We sincerely hope you'll also take advantage of our web sites and the information we've posted there, including a Kaua'i 'Must See & Do' section, listings of all the major Kaua'i places with tips and information for each, discounted Kaua'i activity rates, additional large color photographs of all our favorite Kaua'i places, and a free travel help and support forum where you can ask any questions you have while also helping others by answering their questions.

• *The Lifestyle, People, & Culture*

The Lifestyle: There are a lot of great things about Kaua'i. There are all the unique places, beautiful scenery, smells, beaches, hikes, and oh yes, most of all, the people. If you visit Kaua'i and don't feel at home, you must be doing something wrong for Kaua'i has the most friendly people in the whole country. And given that we are originally from the south, that's saying a lot because most folks from the south think they are THE friendliest. We did too, until we stepped foot on Kaua'i for the first time. And we're not the only ones who think so. Countless other guidebooks, magazines, and popular polls throughout the world show that Kaua'i is time and time again voted near the top of the list when it comes to friendliest place. People smile here, a lot, and they are happy. Strangers say hello when they pass each other, and politeness is a hallmark of the island's identity. It's no

If the scenery alone won't make you smile, the people will.

wonder that Hawaiians themselves will come to vacation on the Garden Isle. Kaua'i is just one of those places you look back and say, "Wow, that was a really special place... everyone was so... well... happy." Aloha!

The People & Culture: Today most anthropologists will tell you that the original settlement of the Hawaiian islands was by Polynesians from the Marquesas Islands around 300-500 AD. This group of early settlers is today believed to be where the legend of the menehune originates. A second wave of settlement followed during the 9th and 10th centuries from Tahiti, radically changing the islands and the culture that existed there.

Mount Wai'ale'ale, meaning "Rippling Waters," is the central mountain of Kaua'i and one of the wettest places on earth. It is the mountain most sacred to the Hawaiian people, being the fount of seven rivers on the island. Atop Wai'ale'ale near the summit is an ancient heiau.

In Hawai'i the new settlers established themselves and found ways to sustain their population. The Tahitians had brought numerous new plants and food sources that would flourish in the Hawaiian Islands. Once established, the Hawaiians had no further need to obtain supplies from their old homelands, and thus underwent centuries of isolation in what is still today the most isolated spot on the planet.

Over time the people developed their own identity and racial bloodlines, essentially evolving individually from their original ancestors and forming a new race, the true Hawaiians. The resemblance however between the Hawaiians and ancient Polynesians in linguistics, characteristics (physically), lifestyle, religious practices, and customs remains close. The original Hawaiians were expert navigators and seamen of brown skin and a large frame. They worshiped and participated in a system known as the "kapu system" that was set down by their chiefs and kahuna (members of the ali'i, or chiefly, class). Their religious system was very deeply tied to nature, and there were hundreds upon thousands of gods in the system. Four main gods were especially important to the Hawaiians, Ku, Kane, Kanaloa, and Lono. Today's modern world is likely most familiar with the goddess Pele and the demigod Maui.

The Hawaiians lived in near complete isolation for a thousand years before their first encounter with white men. It was in 1778 that Captain James Cook, a well known British explorer, stumbled upon the islands much like Columbus had in the Americas centuries before. It was the beginning of great change throughout the islands. Explorers, adventurers, hunters, whalers, trappers, and missionaries would all too soon embark on their own journeys to the newly discovered islands. The role of European and American influence would drastically change the islands forever.

The largest degree of change was precipitated by a shift in culture/religious practices, disease, and the new idea of land ownership. The missionaries' attempts to change the religious ideals of the people was a grand enough change within itself, but the growing presence of foreigners in the islands created medical problems that by modern standards would be a nightmare. In their isolation the Hawaiians were never introduced to many of the diseases the foreigners carried, and within less than a hundred years of Cook's discovery, their population had dropped from 250,000 (possibly even up to a million) to a mere 70,036 by 1853. As the Hawaiian population dwindled, the ability to keep foreigners out became even more of a problem for the native Hawaiians.

A spiritual revolution also began to take place which would ultimately change the religion in Hawai'i to Catholicism. In a final series of defiant acts led by members of the royal family, the basic beliefs of the Hawaiian religion were eventually undermined, and the priests were overthrown. Some argue the spiritual revolution was bound to occur even without the missionaries, as the kapu system was "thrown out" in 1819, a year before the Christian missionaries arrived. The loss of faith in the old gods, intense interest and curiosity about the ways of the people of the United States and Europe, avid interest in learning to read and write, and a desire for spiritual identity brought about a swift adoption of Christianity on the part of the Hawaiians. Now armed with the ability to not only speak a language, but to write it, the islands would soon become the most literate place in the world. There had been no previous written language in Hawai'i until the missionaries' arrival. Everything was passed down by word of mouth. It was for this reason the Hawaiians could recite nearly the entire Bible from memory, an astonishing feat to the missionaries that taught them.

Sacred temples or heiau are symbols of ancient Hawai'i that still exist today. Several can be found along the Wailua River, including Holo-holo-ku seen here.

It was the children of the missionaries' families that would ultimately make the greatest change in Hawai'i. Ideally the families would have returned home as they were supposed to have done but instead stayed on the island and began a practice no Hawaiian had ever heard of, owning land. Over time, Hawai'i was cut into pieces for land-owning residents which to this very day causes great unrest among the Hawaiian people. It was perhaps the military's interests in Pearl Harbor however that would seal the deal as it were. The growing power of those from afar, backed by the military presence, would eventually lead to the overthrow of the Hawaiian monarchy. The rest as they say, is history.

The islands would continue to change over the course of the next century, leading to Hawai'i eventually being annexed by the United States, and ultimately becoming a state. The racial, religious, and cultural background of Hawai'i has changed drastically over that time. Led by the missionaries' descendents, a great agricultural boom occurred in Hawai'i in the early 20th century, bringing more and more immigrants from Japan, China, and the Philippines to work in the growing fields of sugarcane, pineapple, and other large crops. Hawai'i became a melting pot of world cultures, faiths, and customs, which forged a new identity that still holds true today.

Over the last few decades, the Hawai'i of old has re-emerged bringing a great sense of pride to the remain-

Waioli Huiia Church near Hanalei was built in 1929. The mission hall is the oldest surviving church building on the Island of Kaua'i.

ing native Hawaiians. The hula, chant, and old ways are being reborn. The change from an agricultural hearth to a tourist destination has also now exposed Hawai'i to people the world over. A state with a population of only 1.2 million has experienced tourism numbers floating around 7 million in recent years. The influence has been both positive and negative from various points of view. Today, most of the state's residents reside on the island of Oahu, some 60% in Honolulu alone which is the 11th largest city in the United States.

Hawai'i is English speaking, though it is the only state with two official languages, English and Hawaiian. Although Hawaiian, formerly a major means of communication, is all but extinct, it remains in place names, street names, songs, and the local residents liberally sprinkle their speech with words and phrases from the traditional language (see page 220). A "pidgin" English has also formed throughout the state in varying degrees of richness, while some of the older immigrants from Japan and China continue to speak their native tongues. Today, the largest religious groups remain Roman Catholics and Protestants.

A few other quick tidbits of information regarding Hawai'i's culture. If you hear the term "Hawaiian" it is in reference to someone's race only, not where they are. Hawaiian implies they have pure Hawaiian blood in their veins. Locals are typically folks who were born and raised here, but are not necessarily pure Hawaiians. A kama'aina is someone who has lived here a while but typically was not born here. Lastly, the term haole is used for all persons who are white, born here or not.

KAUA'I ITINERARIES

At some point in planning your vacation to Kaua'i it's probably going to hit you, "Wow, this is a lot harder than I thought it'd be... there's so much to do." Welcome to the state where the possibilities for activities and adventures are limitless, to where you'll likely never find yourself bored unless you simply refuse to leave your hotel room. This portion of our guide is here to help you find some focus in planning your trip and should allow you to organize what you want to do into a simple itinerary. Planning your vacation doesn't have to be a chore, and hopefully our recommendations below for the one or two-week vacationer will be of assistance in your own preparation. Our next section, "The Best of Kaua'i - Top 5 Spots," starting on page 73 may also be of assistance to you, especially if you have less than a week on Kaua'i.

We always like to travel by making day-by-day plans, putting the most important up front, and if the weather doesn't cooperate one of those days we just switch that day with another. That way we always get to the important stuff first, and if we have to skip anything, it's the minor places only. The day planners also help us keep some sort of organization to our trips, because until you're really familiar with the island, trying to visit places in a hit-and-miss form will leave you both frustrated and with a lot of miles on your car from all the driving. As an example, attempting to view the Kalalau Lookout and also hike part of the Kalalau trail (even a small part) in the same day just isn't feasible. In reality they are only a few miles apart, but no road connects them on the west side of the island, so you have to drive all the way back around the island to get to the trail head, some 2-3 hours worth of driving. Knowing up front not to make mistakes like this can save you a lot of trouble. One of the biggest mistakes most travelers make is assuming

If you've ever wondered what it felt like to be a bird, to see the world from above, then looking out over Kalalau Valley from Pu'u o Kila lookout might be just the place for you.

they can just breeze around the island at 50-60 miles per hour because, "Hey, it's only an island." Unfortunately, they quickly learn this is not the case, especially on Kaua'i where the speed limits are lower than normal. It's best to plan your trip by grouping spots together. That said, let's look at the suggested one and two-week itineraries.

• *One Week on Kaua'i*

If you're planning to visit Kaua'i for a week, rest assured there is plenty you can do in that time span without missing anything worth seeing. In fact, there isn't a single thing in this book that you can't do, at least in part, during a single week. The goal however is to find balance between relaxation and getting to all the places you want to see. If you're more laid back, want to spend some time on the beaches, swim a few hours each day, etc then seeing every spot in this guidebook probably isn't feasible or likely in a week. On the other hand if you aren't fond of the beaches, prefer the hikes and adventures along the unbeaten path, and don't mind moving at a quick pace, then you might very well be able to complete this entire guidebook in a week's time. Let's try and find a middle point between those two personality types so you can determine what spots are best for your itinerary and time on Kaua'i.

Day 1: Arrival. As we've already suggested, let this be a day to adjust to the islands. Grab a bite to eat, enjoy the sunset that evening, and get to bed early as it has likely been a long day. If you're flying in from another island, as we often do, then some light sightseeing probably won't be a problem once you're set up with your new rental, etc. Just remember, if you're coming from Maui or Oahu things here are very different. Kaua'i's lifestyle pace is nowhere near that of even Maui, much less Oahu. The Big Island is comparable to Kaua'i, so if you're coming from that island, you'll probably not notice too much of a change of pace.

Day 2: This is your first day to really get out and see the island. Our suggestion is to take off towards the north shore and explore all there is to see and do between Lihue and Ke'e Beach. This consists of pages 100-144 of our guidebook. We have also denoted page numbers for each individual spot on the following pages. This is probably going to be one of the highlights of your trip, so it's always a good idea to visit it early on. It'll also help you determine if you want to revisit here later in your trip.

Stops we highly recommend when heading north include Wailua Falls (page 104), Waimea River Overlook and Opaeka'a Falls (page 108), Kilauea Lighthouse (page 126), a morning dip in Queen's Bath (page 132), followed by lunch just further down the road at Hanalei lookout (page 134). Next you'll want to stop at Tunnels Beach for some afternoon snorkeling in the warmest part of the day (page 138). Continuing to the west you'll want to stop at Ha'ena Beach Park and explore the dry cave along with the beach (page 142). After that head west again to the end of the road at Ke'e Beach where you can do some more exploring, check out the start of the Kalalau Trail (but not hike it just yet), and then head back - swimming at Ke'e can be reserved for tomorrow (page 144).

On your way back you might want to visit some of the smaller stops listed along this drive that you skipped on the way up.

Day 3: Heading to the north coast again, this is the day you'll want to hike Kalalau Trail (page 146). We suggest starting the trail no later than 7-8am, as the first two miles will take between four to eight hours, allowing for a side trip to Hanakapi'ai Falls. Plan for each mile to take approximately one hour to hike. If you hike to Hanakapi'ai Beach and turn around, that's four miles and thus four hours (page 152). If you hike inland from Hanakapi'ai Beach to the falls, that's another four miles to add to your total, so you can plan on the hike lasting eight hours. For folks with only a week for vacation, we suggest simply hiking to Hanakapi'ai Beach, turning around and heading back to Ke'e. Once you return you'll have time for swimming at the beach and can enjoy a gorgeous sunset from this vantage point. The colors over the Na Pali coast at sunset as seen from Ke'e Beach are simply indescribable (page 144).

Day 4: Now it's time to head to the west side of the island. We suggest skipping the south part of the island for now and heading directly to our west starting point in Waimea town, see pages 172-176, to begin this trip. From Waimea you'll head north along Waimea Canyon Drive gaining 4,000 feet in elevation over the course of the day (page 178). This is another day you'll want to begin good and early because the drive to the Waimea Canyon area from Lihue alone will take 1-2 hours. Once here, you can explore the many overlooks of Waimea Canyon (page 184) and even do a bit of hiking on the Kukui Trail (page 181) before heading further north. We suggest you finish up with Waimea before 11am if possible, and then head straight for Kalalau Lookout (page 192), or better yet, Pu'u o Kila lookout a mile beyond it (page 192). You might even want to visit these two lookouts first this day, and then come back to Waimea Canyon on the way back down. These two lookouts offer stunningly expansive views of the Kalalau Valley. The best time to view them is probably between 10am-1pm, as the clouds tend to fill them later in the day. This isn't always the case, but we've found that on average it's a good rule of thumb to plan by. If you're into hiking, this might be the day you will want to hike the Pihea/Alaka'i Trail to Kilohana since the trail head is actually at Pu'u o Kila (page 198). You can always return another day, but this is often a challenge for the one week visitor. If you do attempt this hike, be sure to get up extra early this day so that you can begin the trail at 7am or earlier. If the gate at Kalalau Lookout is open, you'll only have an eight mile hike ahead of you, but if the gate is closed, it's a 10-mile round trip hike. Plan for this hike to take at least six hours, or about 40 minutes per mile. If you take the hike you're likely only going to have time to stop at a few places on the return trip, perhaps Waimea Canyon and the Koke'e Museum and Lodge (page 190). These are good stops for folks not partaking in the hike as well. For those who didn't

Polihale Beach State Park in west Kaua'i

opt for the hike, you'll have a lot more things to see after Waimea, the Kalalau Lookout(s), and Koke'e Lodge. You'll want to head back towards Waimea but take Highway 552 when it splits off between mile markers 7 and 6. At the end of this road you'll want to head west towards Polihale Beach (page 208), and once you have explored there it'll likely be near a full day and time to return. If time allows, stops in Waimea, Hanapepe, or even along the south shore (pages 154-170) aren't out of the question.

Day 5: This is a good day to dedicate to the south shore sights, starting on page 154 of our guide. Tree tunnel (page 157), Poi'pu Beach Park (page 166), Spouting Horn (page 162), the National Tropical Botanical Gardens (page 164), and Shipwreck Beach (page 168) are all places to add to your itinerary for this day. After visiting the south shore you may wish to do some shopping in Lihue (pages 100 & 154). Even the Wal-mart has some great souvenirs. In fact, it might be one of the best places on the island to pick up souvenirs, followed by the Coconut Marketplace in Kapa'a (page 120) which would also be good for visiting tomorrow.

Day 6: If this constitutes your last full day on the island, you're likely going to want to take it easy and relax a bit. This is also a good day to consider a "flex" day, one that can be the substituted for a day that was previously rained out, etc. Maybe a helicopter tour of the island would be nice or a short guided tour into Wai'ale'ale Crater (page 114). A visit to the heiaus along Highway 580 in Wailua would be a treat (page 111), as well as a visit to Smith's Tropical Paradise (page 118) and/or a visit up the Wailua River to the Fern Grotto (page 116). You can also revisit any of your favorite places on the north or south shore. If you plan to revisit any sights on the west coast, especially near Waimea Canyon, it might again be a good idea to rise early so you can get started before the crowds arrive near the Canyon. This is also a good day to do more shopping if desired.

Day 7+: As the end of your trip comes near we suggest enjoying the simplest pleasures of Kaua'i. Depending on how much time you have, do what you can these last days, but make sure to relax before your long journey home. Revisiting favorite places not far from Lihue is always a nice treat, as is enjoying a bit of shopping. Make sure you eat some fresh fruit before you leave, and if possible savor that one final sunset (enjoy them every day if you can). Aloha & a Hui Hou, until we meet again.

If you partake in one activity on Kaua'i, then by all means make it a helicopter ride. If you're lucky, Wai'ale'ale might even come out of its misty shroud.

- *Two Weeks on Kaua'i*

If you're lucky enough to have two weeks on the Garden Isle, you're in for a great experience. Not only can you easily view and stop at every spot in this guide, but you can perhaps even do some of them twice, revisiting your favorite spots (and trust us, you'll have favorites you'll want to revisit). The general itinerary for the two-week vacationer isn't that much different from the one-week itinerary. The main difference is the speed and depth of which all activities can be seen and done. A quick read over the one-week section will give a good idea of what to plan on, as you'll likely want to see most places in the same order as recommended above. One huge benefit you'll also have with two weeks is the ability to enjoy more "flex" days. We always want to tell folks they'll have perfect weather in Hawai'i, because most of the time you do have ideal weather. But we have learned that one storm system can really put a damper on things for a day or two. If the island chain is beneath a trough, you can expect that gloomy weather to last even longer. Two weeks provides you more than enough time to see all the best places with ideal weather. Our suggestions below are extensions on the recommendations in the one-week section.

Day 1: Our suggestions for the first day of your journey remain the same as the one-week itinerary. Be sure to take it easy as you are in no rush with two full weeks ahead of you for sightseeing and adventures.

Days 2-3: These days should be devoted to everything (except long hikes) from the east coast to the north shore. You should have plenty of time to explore most every major stop we highlight as well as cover most of the smaller ones. This may be a good time to take the tour into Wai'ale'ale Crater

Ke'e Beach at the end of the road on the north shore.

with a tour guide, and/or take the helicopter ride over the island so you can view it from above before the rest of your trip. This is a good idea when you have a lot of time on an island like Kaua'i, because it sometimes helps you know what you want to go explore later. You've seen it from above, and now you want to see it from the ground. This is a luxury you have with two-week trips but rarely with one. With an open itinerary the last few days of the trip, you have more time to explore and discover things away from the beaten path.

If you can't cover everything in these two days then plan accordingly to return to the north shore at the end of your trip and finish the spots up then. In general, the one-week itinerary covers the highlights of the trip, so we do advise visiting those spots as soon as you can.

Day 4: This is the day for the Kalalau Trail, and unlike one-week visitors you can devote the whole day to the trail. We also recommend the hike inland to Hanakapi'ai Falls for anyone fit and willing enough to make the four-mile trek inland. It's four hours extra time, but it's well worth it for the reward you'll receive in taking the hike. It's not your typical hike and really brings about a sense of exploration on this lush island.

Days 5-7: We always feel it's a safe bet to devote three solid days to Waimea Canyon, Koke'e State Park, and the general west coast. In our opinion it is second only to the Kalalau Trail in beauty and magnificence. With three full days to explore you can do more of the hiking available in the parks here. We recommend you do the light sightseeing the first day and more of the hiking the second and/or third days. There are such a variety of trails avail-

Polihale Beach Cliffs at the end of the road on the west coast.

able here you're sure to find something that suits you. These are perhaps the best trails in all of Hawai'i, so take advantage of them. We only detail a few in our book, but folks at Koke'e State Park Lodge will be more than happy to educate you on the other hikes in the park. The hikes we've already covered we do consider the better of the hikes, but by all means feel free to explore your options. We'd recommend closing out with a visit to Polihale State Park and the other small sights around Waimea town. Between hiking Kalalau, visiting Waimea, viewing Kalalau Lookout(s), and now seeing Polihale you will likely feel a true appreciation for the grandeur behind the Na Pali coast of west Kaua'i.

Day 8: This is the day to explore the south shore sights we noted in the one-week itinerary under 'Day 5.' We have never found ourselves in need of more than one day to explore this part of Kaua'i, and since the weather is almost always fantastic here that is never an issue. One day should suffice for exploring all of south Kaua'i and the surrounding sights.

Days 9-14: There are still 4 or 5 solid days left to your trip, so what should you do with all that time? Well, this is a good chance to participate in various tours, adventures, or even some hikes you perhaps haven't been able to fit in just yet. A few hours on the beach one of these days probably wouldn't be too hard for you to handle, and a few hours of snorkeling at Tunnels Beach just might be good for your soul. This is an ideal time to shop, dine, and relax on the beautiful Garden Isle, let it all soak in. Visit various places where you can get awesome views of the sunset, and enjoy your favorite places again while you still have the chance. Believe us, if you don't, you'll wish you had once you return home. It can be very easy to get "beauty fatigue" while on Kaua'i, and later on you'll wonder how it ever happened. Things that looked "average" on your 13th day will suddenly be "fascinating" and "amazing" again within two months of returning home. Point being, don't take the beauty and experience for granted. It might be hard to believe it, but you actually do start to do that while on a longer vacation to this amazing place. Only when it's gone do you realize your mistake.

Live every day Kaua'i style... and enjoy life. It's a state law that you have to leave your worries behind here. Hopefully after two weeks you will feel you've had the experience that IS Kaua'i. Aloha and A Hui Hou.

Perhaps no other flower on the island gleams with the spirit of aloha like the Bird of Paradise.

THE BEST OF KAUA'I (TOP 5 SPOTS)

If there is one question tour companies, guidebook writers, and travel associates get asked more than anything else, it is probably this, "What are the BEST places to visit on Kaua'i." That's what this section of our guidebook is meant to help answer so that you too can quickly identify the top places to visit on the island. Some visitors have a week or more and can use our itineraries in the previous section (starting on page 60) to their advantage, but others have less time and want to get right to the good stuff. Let's dig in and focus on the very best of Kaua'i, the top 5 places, beaches, waterfalls, hikes/trails, gardens, and activities. We'll start with the grand prize, Kaua'i's number 1 top spot.

- *Kaua'i's Top Spot*

"Spots" are defined as the big things you just have to see, and picking the first one is by far the hardest - how do you pick the absolutely best place to see or visit? Our guidebook is chock-full of great places to see, activities to participate in, beaches to lounge on, trails to hike, and gardens to explore. Luckily for us, the island made it easy and this was a no-brainer, it was the rest that were harder to choose.

#1 Grand Prize: Kalalau Trail - Does any other place on the island catch the true essence of Kaua'i more than this remarkable hike along the stunning Na Pali coast? We can say with a great deal of certainty that this is the one place you have to see. Our reasons are simple. Not only does this trail boast some of the absolute best scenery in all of Hawai'i, but it begins and ends at two of the very best beaches on the island - Ke'e Beach and Kalalau Beach. In between is a variety of waterfalls, side-hikes, beaches, and overlooks that will knock your socks off. Naturally most folks cannot

K **TOP SPOTS** I A U A I

The Kalalau Trail is the grand prize of Kaua'i.

hike the full trail, primarily due to time constraints, but also because of that 22+ mile round trip part. But don't fret, there is a piece of the trail you can still do in a good half-day hike or more and feel like you've experienced Kalalau.

The hike from Ke'e Beach to Hanakapi'ai Beach (page 146) is more than enough to give you a taste of this amazing adventure. If you aren't satisfied when you reach Hanakapi'ai Beach, just head inland for another two miles to Hanakapi'ai Falls (our #3 hike, page 152) cascading down the sheer face of the valley's lush back walls.

If time allows you to make the journey to Kalalau Beach, by all means take the challenge - you'll never forget it.

- *Kaua'i's Top 5 Places*

Selecting five places above all the others is a daunting task, especially on Kaua'i. But after several discussions and a lot of consideration here they are, our top five picks for the best places on the Garden Isle...

#1 Place: Pu'u o Kila Lookout - Given that our grand prize was the amazing Kalalau Trail it should come as no surprise that our number one pick for places is Pu'u o Kila Lookout. Pu'u o Kila is a lookout in west Kaua'i which displays the expansive Kalalau Valley from 4,000+ feet above the beach all the way to the shoreline. No other place can capture your mind, body, and spirit with a sense of awe like Pu'u o Kila.

You can read more on this amazing place starting on page 192.

Pu'u o Kila Lookout scores our number 1 pick for places to visit while on the island of Kaua'i.

K *TOP SPOTS* I
A U A

Wai'ale'ale Crater is our number 2 pick for places.

#2 *Place: Wai'ale'ale Crater* - Our number two pick for places is definitely Wai'ale'ale Crater. You have a few options on how to see this place, so take your pick. You can choose to either explore it on your own by renting a 4x4 and heading up Highway 580 until you reach the "Jurassic Park" gate, view it from a helicopter (our favorite method), or hike into it on foot alone or with a tour.

You can learn more about Wai'ale'ale Crater starting on page 114.

#3 *Place: Waimea Canyon Lookout* - Dubbed, "The Grand Canyon of the Pacific," by Mark Twain, Waimea Canyon Overlook is a place you don't want to miss. The views into the canyon from this overlook are superb and will make you wonder how so much diversity can exist on a single island.

If viewing it from above isn't enough for you, then opt to hike down into the gorge or take a helicopter ride into and above it for some amazing views.

You can learn more about Waimea Canyon Overlook starting on page 184.

#4 Place: Kilauea Lighthouse - There are many things to thrill and delight you at Kilauea Lighthouse and Reserve. For one, the views of this lighthouse from both the overlook and peninsula alike are fantastic. Even better are the abundance of rare birds in the area creating a mecca of sorts for bird watching enthusiasts. And even if bird watching isn't your thing, just witnessing the red and white-tailed tropic birds dancing in the breeze is a beautiful sight to behold.

You can learn more about Kilauea Lighthouse starting on page 126.

#5 Place: Hanalei Valley Scenic Lookout - Rounding out the top five is a picture perfect postcard waiting to happen, the view from Hanalei Valley Overlook. There may be no other overlook on the island quite as easy to get to as Hanalei Overlook. It's right beside the road at the junction of Highway 56 and Highway 560, just beyond Princeville. The views of Hanalei Valley nestled between the surrounding mountains are sure to make you smile.

You can learn more about Hanalei Valley Overlook starting on page 134.

Well there they are, our top five places. A few honorable mentions could be Spouting Horn (page 162) and Poli'ahu Heiau (page 111).

K **TOP SPOTS** I
KAUAI

- *Kaua'i's Top 5 Beaches*

Selecting five beaches above all the rest is as difficult as any other category, but beaches can be especially tough because they come with such a wide array of qualities. Some are better for swimming while others only for lounging. We made up a list of all the beaches on the island, considered several factors, and decided which ones we thought were the most diverse, unique, and interesting to visit. Some are good for swimming, some for snorkeling/scuba, and some just for lounging or sightseeing. So here they are, our top five picks for Kaua'i beaches...

#1 Beach: Ke'e Beach - Taking the top spot at number one on our list is Ke'e Beach on Kaua'i's north shore. This beach is amazing for several reasons, and like most other folks on

When you think of gorgeous beaches in Hawai'i, you're thinking of Ke'e Beach and the stunning view of the Na Pali coast. It ranks in at number 1 on our beach list.

K *TOP SPOTS* I
A U A

79

Whether you like to swim, snorkel, scuba, or just sunbathe, Tunnels beach is the spot for you. Tunnels Beach ranks in at number 2 on our beach list.

Kaua'i, you'll enjoy spending some time here. For one, it's a great beach to do a variety of activities such as swimming, snorkeling, fishing, or just lounging on the beach. The sunsets are jaw-dropping here, and the views of Na Pali to the west are incredible. No other beach has as much to offer as Ke'e Beach.

You can learn more about Ke'e Beach starting on page 144.

#2 Beach: Tunnels Beach - If it's snorkeling you desire on your trip to Kaua'i, then look no further than Tunnels Beach on the north shore of Kaua'i. Tunnels Beach is a great place to see ocean life up close. A large reef, visible even from space, is right offshore creating a mecca for snorkelers and scuba divers alike. And while the ocean views are great, the beach itself isn't half-bad either. It's actually one of the prettiest on the island, and if you can get a decent parking spot (parking is tight for this prized beach), it'll make for a great place to do some sunbathing on a secluded beach that's rarely, if ever, crowded because most folks are in the water.

You can you learn more about Tunnels Beach starting on page 138.

#3 Beach: Po'ipu Beach - Around the island of Kaua'i there are many pristine beaches with long shores of white sand, gentle waves, and gorgeous surroundings. But one thing Po'ipu Beach has nearly year round that the others don't have is great weather. Located on the south shore, Po'ipu Beach is considered "leeward" on the island, thus it often has the best weather conditions for swimming and beach lounging with all the sun you could ever desire. The views are spectacular from this location, with nothing out in front of you but the expansive Pacific Ocean for thousands of miles. Head down the beach toward the west and you'll encounter Kiahuna Beach, doubling your fun with two great beaches right beside one another. All you have to do is cross the road to do some shopping at Po'ipu Shopping Village or tee off for a round of golf at Kiahuna Golf Course.

You can learn more about Po'ipu (and Kiahuna) Beach starting on page 166.

#4 Beach: Polihale Beach - To some of you this may seem like a really strange beach to pick for our top 5, but to others it makes perfect sense. Where else can you walk over

17 uninterrupted miles of sand or see dunes over 100 feet high? Polihale also offers some fantastic views of Ni'ihau offshore and the Na Pali coast. The weather is almost always fantastic here too. Barking Sands Beach is located directly to the left of Polihale and also is a great stop. Access to the beach isn't easy, and the sand can make driving tricky, but when all is said and done this beach still makes the list of top beaches. If nothing else, the spooky feel of it will stay with you for years.

You can learn more about Polihale Beach (including what makes it spooky) starting on page 208.

#5 Beach: Ha'ena Beach - Rounding out the top five is Ha'ena Beach Park on the north shore. While not a great place to swim, it is one of the best beaches on the island to lay back and relax while getting some sun. And if it's not the sun that interests you, but instead the darkness of night, then just head across the road to explore Maniniholo dry cave. Ha'ena Beach Park is truly a unique find. Camping is also available with a permit and the beach has full facilities.

You can learn more about Ha'ena Beach Park starting on page 142.

Well, there they are, our top picks for beaches on the Garden Isle. Kaua'i is simply loaded with beaches, more than any other island in the chain per mile, so make sure you visit at least these top picks. A few other beaches earning honorable mention would be Kalalau Beach, Shipwreck Beach (page 168), and Queen's Bath (page 132).

K TOP SPOTS I
KAUAI

• *Kaua'i's Top 5 Waterfalls*

On a wet island like Kaua'i you'd think picking waterfalls would be an easy task, but you'd be wrong! While Kaua'i is abundant with waterfalls many are no where close to the road and/or publicly accessible. We've attempted to pick falls that you can actually see during your visit, with the exception of one (which you'll have to view by helicopter). So here they are, our top five picks for Kaua'i waterfalls...

Manawaiopuna Falls ranks in at number 1.

#1 Waterfall: Manawaiopuna Falls - Don't hurt yourself trying to pronounce our number 1 pick for waterfalls in Kaua'i, just call it what most folks do, "*Jurassic Park* Falls." The common name that's now come to grace this waterfall originates with the opening sequence of the first *Jurassic Park* movie. It's ironic the movie scene involves a helicopter because that's the only way you're probably going to see this waterfall. Most companies do fly over this waterfall so that you can take a quick snapshot home with you.

We don't detail the falls in our book simply because it is inaccessible, but it's the only one in this top 5 list that you'll only be able to view by air. The rest are all visible by road or trail. This top pick however was just too good to pass up. It's by far the most beautiful waterfall on the island.

#2 Waterfall: Wailua Falls - If you're disappointed that you can't view our number 1 waterfall by vehicle or foot, then we are sure you'll be thrilled with how easily accessible this next one is; it's right beside the road.

Wailua Falls ranks number 2 on our list because if anything is better than one waterfall, it's two. This double-tiered fall is certainly one of the most impressive on the island and is likely the most visited. Its convenient location right outside of Lihue in east Kaua'i makes it a frequent stop for nearly all visitors on the island. From the river above, water cascades 175 feet down the cliff into the giant pool below. The morning sun often creates a rainbow in the mist. For the daring, there is even a hike to the base of the falls.

You can learn more about Wailua Falls on page 104.

Wailua Falls in east Kaua'i ranks in at our number 2 pick for waterfalls.

#3 Waterfall: Hanakapi'ai Falls - Our selection for the number 3 pick is probably going to earn some complaints, as it's another waterfall slightly off the beaten path. (Don't say we didn't warn you about Kaua'i's falls being hard to reach.)

Hanakapi'ai Falls is located four miles from the start of the Kalalau trailhead at Ke'e Beach on the north shore. The first two miles take hikers along the beautiful Kalalau Trail to Hanakapi'ai Beach, and then another two miles take visitors inland to the falls deep in the valley.

If nothing else, look at the bright side, you'll accomplish two feats at one time. You will visit some of the best beaches on the island and hike a portion of the Kalalau Trail (our grand prize pick for Kaua'i) before visiting the falls. You can read more on Hanakapi'ai Falls and the hike to reach it starting on page 146 (trailhead), and 152 (falls).

#4 Waterfall: Opaeka'a Falls - OK, we hear some of you now, "enough of the hard to reach falls already." Don't worry, the next two are right beside the road again and both have easily accessible overlooks. Our number 4 pick for waterfalls is Opaeka'a Falls in east Kaua'i. This beautiful waterfall is active year round and makes for an exquisite photo when the sun is right. The overlook for the waterfall is right beside the road along Highway 580. There is no hiking required, just park and enjoy.

You can learn more about Opaeka'a Falls on page 108.

#5 Waterfall: Waipo'o Falls - We'll admit we had to sorta eke this last one out, but it's the only other falls we can think of that's easily accessible and worth a visit. While the falls can be seasonal and occasionally dry when it hasn't rained in a while, Waipo'o Falls is an absolutely beautiful sight when it is flowing on the eastern walls of the Waimea Canyon. The falls can be seen from several lookouts along the Canyon Drive up Highway 550, but we believe the best lookout by far is at Pu'u Ka Pele.

You can learn more about Waipo'o Falls on page 186.

Well, there you have them, our top 5 picks for waterfalls on the island of Kaua'i. No honorable mention this time. Enjoy!

K *TOP SPOTS* I
KAUAI

- *Kauaʻi's Top 5 Hikes/Trails*

Providing that nearly 90% of Kauaʻi is inaccessible by car, it's no wonder so many folks ask us which trails are the best for their visit. We've thought long and hard about which trails would rank as our top picks. It was a hard task since there are so many wonderful places to explore on foot. However, we feel each of the following top five trails has its own unique qualities that will give you the full Kauaʻi experience. The best trail on the island, Kalalau Trail, was already selected as our "Grand Prize" spot, so make sure to keep that hike in mind when reading over this list. Here's a look at our top 5 picks for Kauaʻi hikes and trails...

#1&2 Hike: Pihea & Alakaʻi Swamp Trail - Our first trail is both our number 1 and number 2 pick for hikes. The reason being, it's actually two unique trails that together offer one amazing hike. You'll begin your journey at the end of the road along Waimea Canyon Drive in Kokeʻe State Park at the Pihea Trailhead. After going two miles along this trail, you'll reach the junction of Pihea and Alakaʻi Swamp Trails. Mind you that the Pihea Trail does continue on from this junction, and that Alakaʻi Swamp Trail has barely begun at this point. Both trails are quite long and even difficult if done in full from start to finish. The hike we are rating as our top pick is actually the best of both trails. It includes a portion of each trail without hiking either to full completion.

From the junction, you'll travel another two miles to the end of Alakaʻi Swamp Trail where you will find your reward, Kilohana Lookout, which offers views all the way to Kilauea Lighthouse along the north shore. On a good clear day, it's enough to easily take your breath away. Some might joke you would lose your breath at about mile four into this hike, but believe us, it's worth it. The hike is close to 8 miles round-trip from Pihea trailhead. If, however, the gate is closed at the Kalalau Lookout, you can add another two miles (round-trip) to that total, thus equaling ten miles. Don't let that number scare you off though, because the trail isn't that bad. We've seen folks of all shapes and sizes make the journey, young and old, big and small. Even if the lookout at the end isn't great due to the weather, the hike itself is a treasure, as it takes you through the heart of the Alaka'i Swamp, the highest swampland rain forest in the world at over 4,000 feet.

You can learn more about the Pihea & Alaka'i Swamp Trail starting on page 198.

Pihea & Alaka'i Swamp Trail might be a long trek through the wilderness of Kaua'i, but it's well worth it. It will leave you with a sense of pride when completing it. It ranks in at our number 1 & 2 pick for hikes on Kaua'i.

Hanakapi'ai Falls is the prize awaiting you at the end of our number 3 pick for hikes, Hanakapi'ai Trail.

#3 Hike: Hanakapi'ai Trail - Technically the hike along Hanakapi'ai Trail is nothing more than a side-trip off the Kalalau Trail. But since this hike is so unique, we simply couldn't resist listing it as our number 3 pick for hikes. Two miles along the rugged Na Pali coast from the trail head of Kalalau is a beach just waiting to be discovered. Day hikers by the dozens make this journey day in and day out. This beach has taken on the name of the valley from which it opens up, Hanakapi'ai Valley.

Heading inland from Hanakapi'ai Beach is a trail to the back of the valley where Hanakapi'ai Falls cascades down the sheer rear valley walls. The trail is harder than the two miles of Kalalau hikers have already completed, but with time, effort, and a sense of adventure, it's worth the extra time. This trail is unique to back-country Kaua'i and is one of our favorites. It's also a lot less "crowded" than the Kalalau Trail.

You can learn more about the Hanakapi'ai Trail starting on pages 146 and 152.

#4 Hike: Kukui Trail - Our number 4 selection is the easiest way to see the "Grand Canyon of the Pacific," from the inside out. The Kukui Trail begins along the western rim of the Waimea Canyon and takes you on an adventure into the heart of the gorge, dropping some 2,000+ feet from the trailhead to the river in the canyon's center. The Kukui Trail offers hikers some incredible views of Waimea Canyon and provides a uniquely different trail from most others on the island. Many of the trails and hikes on Kaua'i are through more lush environments like those expected on a island named the "Garden Isle' - but not Kukui.

Kukui Trail is often dry and even dusty in places, the vegetation drastically different from that found on trails like Hanakapi'ai. Its unique surroundings make it well worth your time and even a mile of the hike will suffice to provide a taste of the experience and give you some amazing photo opportunities.

You can learn more about Kukui Trail on page 181.

#5 Hike: Wai'ale'ale "Jungle" Trail - Our selection for the number 5 hike on Kaua'i is one that you can do one of two ways. The first being, you rent an SUV for the day to reach the trailhead and then proceed from there. The second being, you keep your regular rental and hire a good tour company to take you to the trailhead and guide you along it. Now, usually we're the type of travelers who like to go it alone and do it ourselves, but Wai'ale'ale is different. Sometimes it pays to have a tour guide who knows the history, legends, and surroundings better than you ever could. Not to mention the fact that you won't have to risk damaging your rental car on the rugged road. The Wai'ale'ale Trail isn't strenuous or even remotely difficult. It is however nothing short of amazing. It gives you the rare opportunity to gaze into Wai'ale'ale's crater from the ground, to see the walls of the crater covered with waterfalls of every shape and size. Many have dubbed this wall "the weeping wall" or " the wall of tears." Whatever you call it, the hike is well worth your time and the money for a guided tour.

You can read more about Wai'ale'ale Trial on page 114.

A few other trails we'd easily give honorable mention to are the Nu'alolo Trail, Nu'alolo Cliff Trail, and Awa'awapuhi Trail.

- *Kaua'i's Top 5 Gardens*

We're not sure you can actually visit an island called the "Garden Isle" and not visit any gardens. It just wouldn't be a Kaua'i vacation otherwise. Ironically though, gardens, or at least well-maintained gardens, are fairly rare on the island. That leaves us with a limited selection which makes the choices fairly easy. We've detailed each of these gardens in our guide, and at least one of them is worth a visit if you have the time and can afford it. Be forewarned that some of these gardens are quite expensive to visit. Here's a look at our top 5 picks for Kaua'i gardens...

#1&2 Garden: National Tropical Botanical Garden - Our selection for the top garden in Kaua'i is actually two gardens in one, McBryde Gardens and Allerton Gardens. Together they make up one of the most beautiful gardens in all

The NTBG is our number 1 & 2 pick for Kaua'i Gardens.

K *TOP SPOTS* I
KAUAI

This photograph of Smith's Tropical Paradise shows less of the garden and more of the birds, but that's half the fun at Smith's. Smith's Paradise ranks in as our number 3 pick for Gardens on Kaua'i.

of Hawai'i, the National Tropical Botanical Garden (NTBG), thus earning our pick for both the number 1 and number 2 garden. Located in south Maui, this garden is definitely worth a visit. The only downside is the price, $30 or more a person (subject to change).

You can learn more about the National Tropical Botanical Garden starting on page 164.

#3 Garden: Smith's Tropical Paradise - Some might call us "bird brained" for selecting Smith's Paradise as our number 3 pick, and we might just agree with them - more on that in a second. Smith's Tropical Paradise isn't your typi-

cal garden, it has more than just walkways lined with exotic flowers. It also has a variety of fruit trees and animals to enjoy during your visit. Plus, you can learn about Polynesian history through several educational displays. But why "bird brained?" Simple, it's the birds inside the garden. There are hundreds of them, and they'll follow you around the park (especially if it's not crowded during your visit). They are definitely one of the most entertaining aspects of the garden. Smith's is always a safe bet, and with low admission costs, it's good for couples and families alike.

You can learn more about Smith's Tropical Paradise on page 118.

#4 Garden: Limahuli Garden - Located on the north shore, Limahuli Garden is both a garden and history lesson combined into one place. Nearly 17 acres of publicly accessible gardens make this a real treat to those that visit each day, plus the garden has the ruins of taro terraces dating back a century or more. The garden is also now a part of the National Tropical Botanical Garden, so if the price of the NTBG in south Kaua'i is too expensive for your taste, you can still visit Limahuli and get the experience of one of the NTBGs.

You can learn more about the Limahuli Garden starting on page 140.

#5 Garden: Na 'Aina Kai Botanical Garden - A great garden, and well known for its bronze statues. Unfortunately the price deters most folks, up to $75 a person. Worth a visit, if you can afford the high cost.

You can learn more about Na 'Aina Kai on page 124.

K *TOP SPOTS* I
A U A

• *Kaua'i's Top 5 Activities*

If you visit Hawai'i then it's almost a given that you have to participate in at least one good activity. Even the go-it-alone crowd, like us, should take time out for one good adventure with a tour company. And on Kaua'i that rule is especially true because some of the best things to do on the island can't be done alone. On any given Hawaiian island there are hundreds if not thousands of activities to choose from, so selecting five above all that exist is a daunting task. We've attempted to select activities that won't stretch your budget too far and are well worth any money you do spend. Plus, we've selected activities that will provide you with a diverse array of experiences. If it were up to us, we'd try each and every one of them during our visit. Here's a look at our top 5 picks for Kaua'i activities...

A helicopter ride over Kaua'i is our number 1 pick for Kaua'i activities. The views are outstanding.

#1 Activity: Helicopter Tour - If there is a single thing you pay high dollar for in Kaua'i then by all means let it be this one activity. We won't lie, it's going to cost you some fairly big bucks, and if you've ever taken a helicopter tour before you already know just what we mean. But it's definitely worth it. With so much of the island out of reach by car or even trail, the only true way to see this hidden island is by air. There are numerous helicopter companies available for you to choose from, some of which will even video record your flight for you to take home. We highly suggest researching each company before selecting a flight. Nearly every company now has a website, so definitely do your homework to look for the best flights and deals.

A few tips to consider for helicopter flights:

1.) Don't book a tour under 60 minutes, otherwise everything will go by too quickly. You get what you pay for.

2.) Research the helicopter models you'll fly in. Make sure they are what you want for photos, space, etc.

3.) Check with the company of choice to see who your pilot will be and how many flight hours they have. Several companies like to advertise the number of flying hours logged by the company's owner. Unfortunately, that tells you absolutely nothing about the flying experience of the employees. Not every pilot who qualifies for a helicopter license has had extensive experience with Kaua'i's wilderness terrain.

4.) Ask about a refund policy. Choppers tend to fly rain or shine, so it never hurts to ask what happens if the weather ruins your sightseeing on a flight.

K A U A I
TOP SPOTS

Wai'ale'ale Crater as seen from the "blue hole" is a remarkable experience that earns our number 2 ranking for activities on Kaua'i.

#2 *Activity: Wai'ale'ale "Jungle" Tour* - This is the same as our number 5 recommendation under hikes, the Wai'ale'ale Jungle Hike. In this case we're talking about the tour aspect only, not the do-it-yourself hike. Wai'ale'ale is truly the rare gem of the island, so a trip to near the crater on foot is one of a kind. Most helicopter rides will whisk you into the crater and out again, making your whole experience with the wettest spot on earth but a few seconds. A tour, however, gives you the chance to see the crater up close from the ground.

You can learn more about this activity and even book a tour on our web site at:

www.hawaiianstyletravel.com/KauaiGuide/Guide815.htm

#3 Activity: Fern Grotto Tour - If you're looking for a unique activity on Kaua'i, then our number 3 pick might just be what you're looking for, the Fern Grotto Tour. From the docks in Wailua you'll take a ride up the Wailua River in an open-air river boat. The journey is narrated live by local Kaua'i residents. Some folks may even get a quick hula lesson on their trip up the river. Don't be surprised if you pass by kayakers and even some people water skiing on the way. Eventually you enter one of the back tributaries of the Wailua River, nearly two miles from your starting point. Another dock awaits you at the Grotto. It is here you'll discover the enchanting Fern Grotto and gardens. No reservations are needed for this tour, just show up at the docks 15+ minutes before departure and you're good to go. Costs for the tour are $20 for Adults and $10 for keiki's (children); prices subject to change.

You can learn more about this activity, including where to purchase your tickets in Kaua'i, starting on page 116.

You can also purchase tickets and book your tour online via our web site at:

www.hawaiianstyletravel.com/KauaiGuide/Guide56.htm

#4 Activity: Na Pali Sunset Tour - If the fern grotto isn't exactly the boat tour you're looking for then maybe our number 4 pick will be more to your liking. Imagine this, you sail along the Na Pali coastline as the sun sinks below the horizon, the shadows of the Pali ridges reaching deep inside the valleys. Lush surroundings, sea caves, and beautiful coastal views are accompanied by a warm meal on a 65+ foot catamaran. As far as boat tours go on the island, you really can't get much better than a tour along the stunning Na Pali Coast. It's one thing to hike Na

Pali, and another to view it by air, but the thrill of seeing it from the ocean the way the original Hawaiians did is a treasure you'll never forget. Plus, you'll have the advantage of seeing it atop a guided motor boat with no oars to row. Who can argue with that?

You can learn more about this activity and even book your tour on our web site at:

www.hawaiianstyletravel.com/KauaiGuide/Guide818.htm

#5 *Activity: Snorkel Tour* - Our last activity is one you can choose to do alone or with a tour group, it's really up to you. We think you can do it yourself as easily as you can with a guided tour, plus you'll save yourself some money in the process. Our number 5 pick for the Garden Isle is snorkeling, and in this case, it's at Tunnels Beach (our number 2 pick for top beaches as well). The parking at Tunnels Beach isn't bad and the snorkeling is phenomenal, especially in the summer when the north shore is less prone to large swells and waves. The reef is so large you can even see it in NASA photos taken from the space shuttle. It's a snorkeler's dream come true. If snorkeling at Tunnels isn't quite as adventurous as you'd like, you can always opt for a guided tour of other snorkel locations, including along the Na Pali Coast.

A bit of research online might be of use in finding the ideal company if you choose to go that route. You might also want to check inside the drive guide you receive with your rental for coupons to various snorkel tours. Then simply book the tour once you've arrived.

Well there you have them, our top 5 places, beaches, waterfalls, trails, gardens, and activities on the Garden Isle of Kaua'i. Hopefully these lists will help you determine which spots you absolutely must see.

We sincerely hope that our itineraries and top 5 lists will serve as a general guide of the most amazing places the island has to offer, so that all visitors, on a tight schedule or not, can immediately identify which spots to visit first and for how long. We do feel that all the spots listed in our guidebook are the high end of available attractions on the island of Kaua'i, but it is by no means a complete list. A published work containing details on all of Kaua'i's attractions, adventures, hikes, and tours would easily fill several volumes of books. So with no further ado, let's take a look at the island stop by stop, mile by mile. Our journey begins on the east coast of Kaua'i in Lihue. As always, if you'd prefer to start your journey in another area of Kaua'i, just flip to that page to begin. Aloha to the Garden Isle, and mahalo nui for letting us be your guide.

K A U A I
E A S T

EAST KAUA'I - NORTH LIHUE
Mile Marker 0 – Lihue on Highway 56 (★★★☆☆)

Lihue is the proverbial brain of Kaua'i, the county seat, and the largest city on the island. It is where your journey to Kaua'i began, in Lihue airport, and thus Lihue serves as a solid starting point for our guide in Kaua'i. We'll actually start from Lihue twice, the first time we'll head north along the east coast (Highway 56) until we reach the north shore at Kilauea. This will allow us to visit both the east and north shore detailing all the major highlights along the way.

Then after visiting the north shore we'll start here again in Lihue and head south along Highway 50 exploring the south shore until we reach Waimea Town. At that point, we'll explore the various highways located on that part of the island by first heading across Waimea Town towards

Lihue marks the beginning of your journey on Kaua'i.

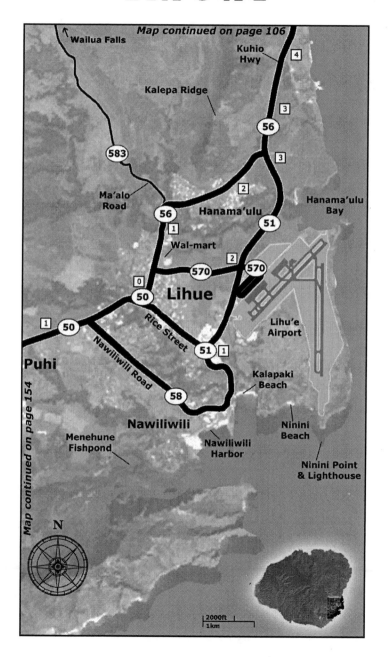

Map continued on page 106

Wailua Falls

Kuhio
Hwy

4

Kalepa Ridge

3

56

583

3

Ma'alo
Road

2

56

Hanama'ulu

Hanama'ulu
Bay

1

51

Wal-mart

2

570

570

0

50

Lihue

Rice Street

Lihu'e
Airport

1

50

51

1

Puhi

Nawiliwili Road

Kalapaki
Beach

58

Nawiliwili

Ninini
Beach

Menehune
Fishpond

Nawiliwili
Harbor

Ninini Point
& Lighthouse

Map continued on page 154

N

2000ft
1km

EAST KAUAI

To many people, Lihue is a small and simple coastal town. It is actually the largest and busiest on the island of Kaua'i.

Polihale to the end of Highway 50. Then we'll backtrack to Waimea Town and head north along Highway 550 towards Waimea Canyon and Koke'e State Park. To put all of this in perspective you may want to see the full island map on page 18.

There are a few things we want to mention as we begin in Lihue. First, take a moment to observe the full size of Lihue. The airport is the only official way on or off the island by air, and the terminal also serves as the heliport for all the island's helicopter tour companies. There is plenty of shopping. You'll find the only Wal-Mart on the island in Lihue (before mile marker 1 on Highway 56).

K_A^{E A S T}U_AI   103

Lihue is an area you'll likely want to avoid during the "rush" hour and the early morning when possible, as traffic can get pretty congested in the city, especially directly to the north near Kapa'a. The county has attempted to alleviate this problem by using two lanes of Highway 56 (Kuhio Highway) as contra-flow lanes from 6:30am-8:30am on weekdays. If you're not used to contra-flow make sure you pay close attention to the road signs erected during this period. Depending on which way you are traveling, you may have either lost or gained a lane to drive in.

As for the rest of Lihue, we'll leave it for you to discover and explore on your own. You likely won't spend a lot of time there, but definitely make sure to check it out before you leave. For now, we'll begin our journey north along Highway 56.

The Lihue airport also serves as the heliport for all the island's helicopter tour companies.

EAST

WAILUA FALLS
Mile Marker 1 – Off Highway 56 (★★★★★)

As we begin our journey up Highway 56 on Kaua'i's east coast we're going to start with a real treat. If you've ever dreamed of seeing a double-tiered waterfall, then you're about to bring that dream to life at gorgeous Wailua Falls. Right after mile marker 1 there will be a road on your left, Ma'alo Road (Highway 583), accompanied by a sign pointing you in the direction of the falls. Take the short drive up this road which will end at a parking lot overlooking the falls. If you're lucky, the sun will be at the right angle, and you'll get a beautiful rainbow extending out from the base of the falls in the mist.

Wailua Falls is approximately 175 feet high and drops into a pool over 30 feet deep. Don't even think of diving off this waterfall though, the leap can be, and has been proven, fatal. Ancient Hawaiians once learned as much when proving their manhood (or foolishness, take your pick). If you have to get

K^{EAST}AUAI

Check out this view of Wailua Falls as seen from above.

to the bottom of the falls (which, mind you, the county advises against) then there are two trails that make the journey quite a bit safer than jumping off. You'll notice the first trail by the guard rail at the end of the parking lot. This is the steeper and often muddier trail. We advise against using this trail at all costs. If you head a little over a quarter mile back down the road however you'll find a easier, less steep, trail. It's longer than the first trail, but it's a lot easier to hike, though please keep in mind again that the county advises against the hike. The signs erected at each trail are a testament to this fact.

In our opinion, the falls are best seen safely from above at the overlook. Please don't throw rocks and other items into the pool below (which likely will be partially out of view). County warning or not, some people DO hike to the bottom of the falls and likely won't like being showered with anything but water.

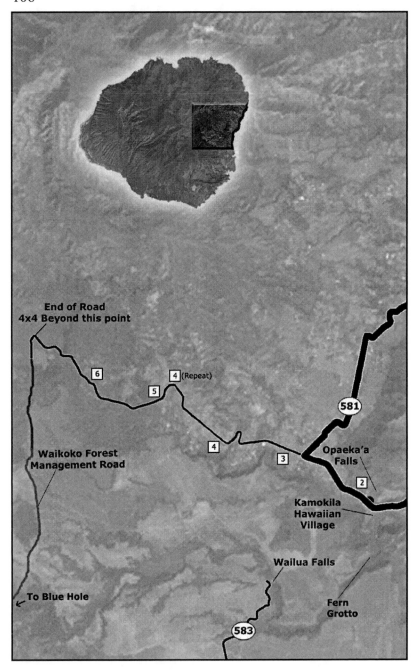

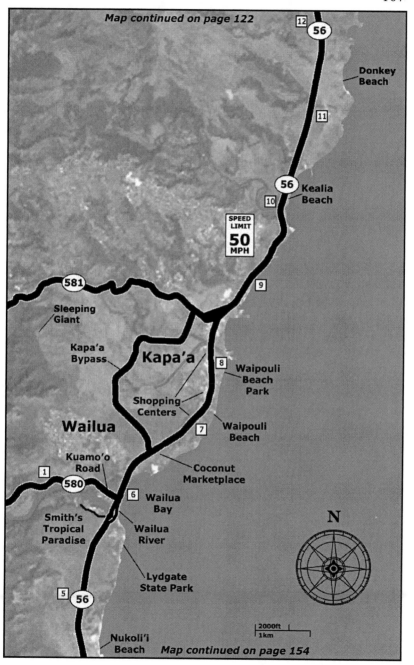

Map continued on page 122

12
56

Donkey
Beach

11

56
Kealia
Beach

10

SPEED
LIMIT
50
MPH

9

581

Sleeping
Giant

Kapa'a
Bypass

Kapa'a

8
Waipouli
Beach
Park

Shopping
Centers

Wailua

7
Waipouli
Beach

Kuamo'o
Road

1

580

Coconut
Marketplace

Smith's
Tropical
Paradise

6
Wailua
Bay

Wailua
River

Lydgate
State Park

N

5
56

Nukoli'i
Beach

2000ft
1km

Map continued on page 154

K A U A I
EAST

OPAEKA'A FALLS & WAILUA RIVER LOOKOUT
Mile Marker 1 – Highway 580 (★★★★☆)

After you reach Highway 56 again, you'll want to take a left and continue north. If you're traveling through this area in rush hour traffic, expect some congestion. The low speed limits on the island, combined with the fact most roads are only two lanes, can cause traffic to be a headache in places throughout the day, especially at peak tourist times in the summer. In any event, we're heading north towards the Wailua River area to our next stop.

Right before mile marker 6 you'll cross over Wailua River. Make sure you're in the left lane as the right splits off onto its own unique little bridge. You'll be looking for Kuamo'o Road (Highway 580) on your left. Head up Kuamo'o Road until you see a pullout for Opaeka'a Falls on your right, shortly before the second mile marker.

Opaeka'a Falls as seen from the lookout on Highway 580.

From this overlook, you can get a spectacular view of 150+ foot Opaeka'a Falls. The falls are at their best in full sunlight (late morning usually). So if you visit on a cloudy day, definitely try to return at a sunnier hour. Best of all, the falls are flowing year round. You're always certain to see it in action. If you're wondering about the origin of the name Opaeka'a, it dates back to days when shrimp roamed the river and were seen rolling in the turbulent waters at the base of the falls. 'Opae' is the Hawaiian word for 'shrimp', and 'ka'a' means 'rolling.'

There is a "hidden" trail to the falls right around the two mile marker past the guardrail, and it's more worn now than it was in previous years. We advise against this trail, mainly because you have to cross a fairly deep stream, walk down

Wailua River lookout across from Opaeka'a falls is yet another amazing scenic lookout.

a steep hill, and then get out again. The trail is supposedly all on state owned land, but it is not maintained and could easily be closed if any incidents occur. Like back at Wailua Falls, the overlook remains the best and safest way to view the falls.

Across the road from the falls is another lookout over the Wailua River Valley. From this overlook you can get a good look at where *Raiders of the Lost Ark* was filmed, along with other big-name movies like *Jurassic Park* and *Outbreak*. If you look to the right you can also get a good look at Kamokila Hawaiian Village. The turnout to the village is right past the overlooks, and entry is $5.

POLI'AHU HEIAU & WAILUA RIVER OVERLOOK
Mile Marker 1 – Highway 580 (★★★☆☆)

Before you leave Opaeka'a Falls, we thought we'd introduce you to one of Kaua'i's most legendary structures located just across the road. Here you'll find an ancient heiau or place of worship. Poli'ahu Heiau is actually one of seven stretching along the Wailua River from the ocean to the top of Wai'ale'ale a few miles inland where the river is born. The Wailua River has always been very sacred to the Hawaiian people and continues to be until this day. While Poli'ahu isn't the largest heiau on the island (Malae across the river is the largest), it is a very impressive structure and a mystical place to visit. Don't confuse it with the smaller Holoholo-ku Heiau a half mile up Hwy 580. Poli'ahu will be in a larger open area with an overlook of the Wailua River. There are also Hawai'i Visitor Bureau signs marking the heiaus.

K A U A I
EAST

The grounds of Poli'ahu heiau also contain this magnificent view of the Wailua River as it flows toward the ocean.

It is said that the Menehune were responsible for the construction of most of the heiaus in this area, Poli'ahu included. The Menehune were a group of small legendary people who were said to build great things in the span of a single night's time. From ditches, ponds, to heiaus their work can be seen on Kaua'i to this very day. In reality, the Menehune may likely have been the first Hawaiians who arrived from the Marquesas Islands around the sixth century. The Menehune legends come from other settlers who reached Hawai'i six or seven hundred years later from the Islands of Tahiti. Scholars have concluded that this second wave of immigrants may have defeated the descendants of the original Marquesans, driving them north from the Big Island to Kaua'i where they made their last stand. Only later did they emerge in their elfin guise.

Exploring Highway 580 is a great way to get close to an ancient Hawaiian heiau like Poli'ahu (above) and Holo-holo-ku (below). A few feet up the road from Holo-holo-ku is the ancient birthstone where Kaua'i kings were born.

WAIʻALEʻALE HIKE TO THE 'BLUE HOLE'
Waikoko Forest Management Road (★★★★★)

At the end of Highway 580, Kuamoʻo Road will turn into Waikoko Forest Management Road. We believe for most travelers this is a drive that should be done only by those with 4x4 vehicles and offroading experience. The drive beyond the paved highway is very rough, bumpy, often muddy, and dangerous in spots (especially when crossing streams). There are some occasions when a standard rental car could make the trip, but until you get back on the road you won't know, so it's not something we advise people to just leave to chance. Don't fret though, you can still get to the blue hole and view what many call the "Wall of Tears" of Mount Waiʻaleʻale by taking a guided tour. During our last visit we decided to give the tour a try and really

The view from the "blue hole" is one of the most gorgeous on the island. The views of Waiʻaleʻale Crater are both surreal and stunning.

enjoyed ourselves. We think you will too. The tours head inland beyond Kuamo'o Road and the Wailua Reservoir to the Keahua Arboretum. Shortly after you pass the arboretum you'll quickly see why it was a good idea to take the tour versus using your rental car. The trail crosses streams and winds through the dense forest to the, "Gate," used in *Jurassic Park*. After parking at the gate, you'll stroll for about half an hour past wild flowers and gorgeous vistas to the "Blue Hole," where water is diverted into the irrigation system of Lihue Plantation. The streams of water cut through the lush greenery of the crater wall like tears streaming down a face, hence its other nickname, the wall of tears. There is a total of about 3 miles of walking involved in this tour which is operated in the Wailua Forest Management Area, under a permit issued by the Na Ala Hele Trail Access Program of the Department of Land and Natural Resources. You can learn more on our travel web site:

www.hawaiianstyletravel.com/KauaiGuide/Guide815.htm

K A U A I
EAST

WAILUA RIVER & FERN GROTTO TOUR
Road to Smith's Tropical Paradise (★★★☆☆)

After seeing all the sights along Highway 580 we suggest you turn right back onto Highway 56. We're going to backtrack a second to the other side of the river. The Wailua River is said to be the only navigable river in Hawai'i (depending on how you define navigable). In the case of taking a boat a few miles inland to a lovely mecca of ferns and tropical plants, it means Wailua River. The first road on Highway 56 after pulling off Highway 580 is the road to Smith's Tropical Paradise (that's the best name to give it, there doesn't appear to be a real name for the road).

There will be a ticket booth on the right where you'll want to stop and purchase your ticket for the trip up the Wailua River. The price is only $20 and well worth it. Tours depart frequently throughout the day and are run by Smith's

Motorboat Service. You can also opt to kayak up the river, but the tour is a much easier route for most visitors. This ticket booth should have a schedule of tours for each day, except Sundays.

The boat will take you three miles up the Wailua River and make a visit to the famous Fern Grotto. As of our last visit it was still under major renovation, so when they complete the work, it should be even better. It really hasn't been the same since Hurricane Iniki in 1992. Many old photographs show what the Grotto will hopefully look like again one day.

The Fern Grotto is a large natural amphitheater with hundreds of ferns draped from it. The gardens leading up to the amphitheater are full of tropical plants and flowers, including the incredible split-leaf philodendrons or swiss-cheese plant - one of our favorites (the vegetation at the bottom of the photo on the previous page is the split-leaf). It is actually native to Mexico, but it makes for a lovely addition to Hawai'i's jungles. The tour is about 30 minutes up the river in the large passenger boats, usually accompanied by entertainment, mele (song), and dance. The visit to the Grotto itself is usually between 30-45 minutes. The Fern Grotto is also a popular place for weddings, and many ceremonies take place there, several on the same day in some instances.

Once you've taken the tour and experienced the Grotto, turn left out of the dock parking lot. Smith's Tropical Paradise is located beside the dock a little bit down the road.

SMITH'S TROPICAL PARADISE GARDEN
Beyond Boat Docks - Off Hwy 56 (★★★☆☆)

Right beyond the Wailua River Boat docks is Smith's Tropical Paradise. If you aren't looking for it, you might not even notice it. It's sort of tucked away in the background. But don't let it go unnoticed on your trip, because it's a very unique garden that is sure to please your entire family. Smith's Tropical Paradise is a lush 30-acre botanical and cultural garden, and the low cost (the lowest we've found for a decent garden on the island) makes it one of Kaua'i's leading attractions. Each day visitors stroll along the winding paved pathways of the garden surrounded by various plants and beautiful flowers. All-in-all there is about a mile of path to walk in the garden, but if you aren't up for walking, just take the tram ride narrated by one of their friendly guides.

Smith's Tropical Paradise has earned its name. If this isn't paradise, we don't know what is.

K<small>EAST</small>AUAI

Beyond it's low cost and excellent condition, one of the best things about this garden are the birds. There may not be another location on Kaua'i where you can get so much attention from the local birds of the island. Here you'll find exotic peacocks, zebra and spotted doves, wild chickens, and even the rare and endangered "singing tree duck." Many of the birds will follow you around the walkways or even flock to you when fed. Smith's Paradise also has other animals within the garden, including the intimidating Hawaiian boar. Don't worry, they are caged. Various fruit trees also grace the garden, and if you visit in the spring or early summer you'll be treated with Plumeria blossoms. Plus, you can learn about Polynesian history through several educational displays.

The Botanical and Cultural Gardens are open between 8:30 a.m. and 4:00 p.m. The cost has fluctuated, though we've typically paid about $6 per person, less for keikis (children).

For more information you can visit their web site at:

www.SmithsKauai.com/paradise.html

K $\overset{E\ A\ S\ T}{A\overset{}{U}A}$ I

KAPA'A TOWN & SLEEPING GIANT
Mile Marker 7 - Highway 56 (★★☆☆☆)

As we mentioned earlier, depending on what time of day you are traveling along Highway 56 it can become pretty congested. There is a bypass road around Kapa'a, which looks to remain open beyond the "temporary" time line originally set for it. As of press time the bypass was still in use and has shown no sign of being shut down. View the map on page 107 for a better look.

As you drive through Kapa'a make sure to keep your eyes open for the Sleeping Giant on the ridge. Legend tells of the time he built a great heiau for the people of Hawai'i, ate too much and then fell asleep, which is what he continues to do today. The photo below shows what you're looking for. Some people see him, some don't. His head is to the left in the photo below.

Kapaʻa is quickly turning into the resort area of the island, and thus has become quite a hot-spot for locals and tourists alike. One of the best places on the island to shop is the Coconut Marketplace located half way between mile markers 6 and 7 on Highway 56. The marketplace will be on your right. After you pass mile marker 7 the real heart of Kapaʻa is before you with all its shops, stores, and restaurants. The Kauaʻi Village Shopping Center is on the left about 4/10 mile past mile marker 7 and the Kapaʻa Shopping Center (including a post office) is located right before mile marker 8 on the left.

There are several beaches on this side of the island, but none are as nice or notable as those found on the north shore. Kapaʻa Beach Park (seen below) is heavily used by locals and kite surfers when the wind is right. Lately, it has also become increasingly popular with island visitors because of its proximity to their resorts in Kapaʻa.

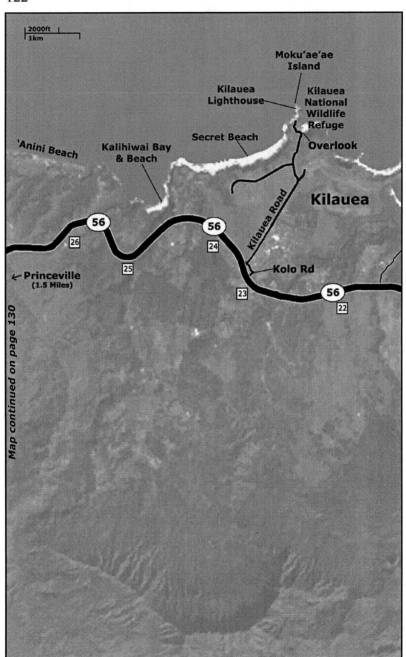

2000ft
1km

Moku'ae'ae
Island

Kilauea
Lighthouse

Kilauea
National
Wildlife
Refuge

Secret Beach

Overlook

'Anini Beach

Kalihiwai Bay
& Beach

Kilauea

Kilauea Road

56

56

26

24

25

Kolo Rd

23

56

22

← Princeville
(1.5 Miles)

Map continued on page 130

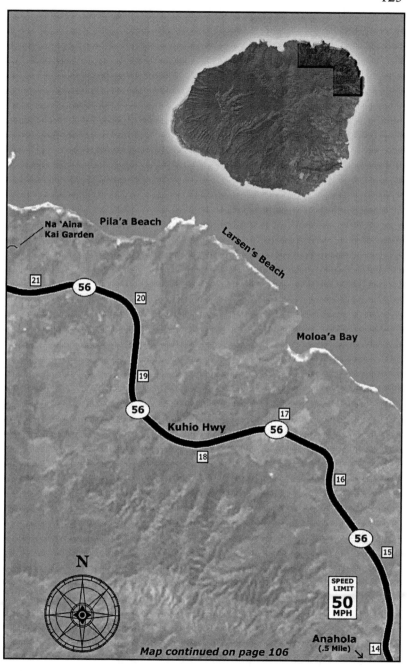

Na 'Aina Kai Garden

Pila'a Beach

Larsen's Beach

Moloa'a Bay

21

56

20

19

56

Kuhio Hwy

17

56

18

16

56

15

N

SPEED LIMIT 50 MPH

Map continued on page 106

Anahola (.5 Mile)

14

NORTH SHORE - NA 'AINA KAI GARDEN
Mile Marker 21 - End of Wailapa Road (★★★★☆)

As you head north make sure to make a quick stop between mile markers 21 and 22 at Na 'Aina Kai Botanical Gardens located at the end of Wailapa Road. Founded in 1982 by Ed and Joyce Doty. The name means "Lands by the Sea" in Hawaiian and is a continuously evolving garden that is unique among all the other botanical gardens on the island.

The garden spans some 240 acres and is a living mosaic of 13 diverse and bountiful gardens. Here you'll also discover a 110-acre hardwood plantation, 45-acre fruit orchard, moss and fern draped canyon, and a lovely tranquil sand beach. The garden is also well known throughout the world for its 70+ bronze sculptures, which remain one of the nation's largest collections.

In the garden you'll also find a large garden maze, desert garden, several orchid plants, and bog plant house.

Today the garden can be toured Tuesday-Thursday throughout the year. All tours are guided and all visitors must be at least age 13 and over. The tours are a bit pricey but said to be well worth it by those who visit throughout the year. You can expect to spend around $25-$75 per person, or on average about $35 for the standard 3-hour tour that is most often taken. Call in advance to make reservations.

You can obtain their phone number, contact information, and learn more about the garden at their web site:
www.naainakai.org/

The amazing variety of bronze statues inside Na 'Aina Kai Botanical Gardens is worth the money alone. The collection is one of the largest in the United States today.

KILAUEA LIGHTHOUSE & WILDLIFE REFUGE
Mile Marker 23 - Kilauea at Highway 56 (★★★★★)

As you continue to drive north past Kapa'a you'll pass through the town of Anahola around mile marker 13. Continue north along the Kuhio Highway (Hwy 56) until you come to Kolo Road shortly after mile marker 23. The road will be on your right. After you have turned onto Kolo Road you are going to want to take Kilauea Road makai (towards the ocean) to Kilauea Lighthouse and the national wildlife refuge that has been set up there. You have also now officially entered North Kaua'i.

Before heading down to the lighthouse parking lot on the peninsula, take a moment to stop at the upper lot and view the lighthouse from the overlook. Then continue on down to the lower parking lot.

The Kilauea Lighthouse is merely a dot against the ocean background from this view.

K*NORTH*AUAI

Kilauea Lighthouse is the northernmost point of the main Hawaiian Islands. The lighthouse was built in 1913 with the largest hand blown clamshell lens in the world. It was later replaced with a beacon in the 1970's. The lighthouse is open to look around on the ground level. Today the lighthouse remains one of Kaua'i's most popular attractions. Native vegetation and an informative visitor center attracts thousands of tourists to this site to bird watch, view the sweeping cliff and ocean vistas, and revel in Kaua'i's past.

Nearby is the Kilauea Point National Wildlife Refuge, home to a diverse population of nesting seabirds and the only such sanctuary in the islands. Residents include red-footed boobies, the Laysan albatross, the red and white-tailed tropic bird, and the great frigate bird with its 8-foot wingspan. During certain seasons green-sea turtles, humpback whales, and dolphins can be seen frolicking in the waters. The refuge is open daily 10am - 4pm (subject to change).

Crater Hill, landward from the lighthouse, is part of an extinct volcano that looms above the refuge and is open to hikers. From this hill are terrific views of the North Shore coast and the seabird nests.

Moku'ae'ae Islet, pictured above, is just offshore from the peninsula. It is a bird sanctuary and often home to the Hawaiian monk seal which may be seen lounging in the sun near the shoreline.

The Nene (Hawaiian State Goose) can be found around the peninsula too. We've been told by some folks that they don't fly as far north and west as Kaua'i, but we've seen more on Kaua'i than any other island.

One of the highlights of Kilauea Lighthouse is the wildlife refuge for birds. You can observe the birds in their natural habitat nesting (like seen above) or watch the tropic birds "dance" in the wind all around the lighthouse.

130

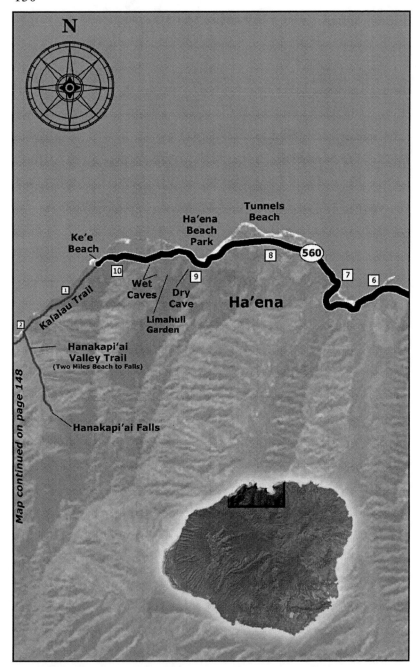

N

Map continued on page 148

Ke'e
Beach

Ha'ena
Beach
Park

Tunnels
Beach

560

8

7

6

10

9

Wet
Caves

Dry
Cave

Ha'ena

Limahuli
Garden

1

Kalalau Trail

2

Hanakapi'ai
Valley Trail
(Two Miles Beach to Falls)

Hanakapi'ai Falls

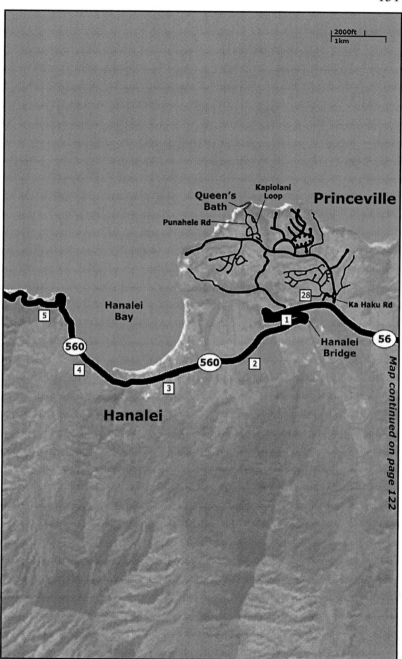

Map continued on page 122

QUEEN'S BATH IN PRINCEVILLE
Mile Marker 27 - Highway 56 (★★★★☆)

As we continue north on Highway 56 the road begins to move more toward the west than north. Our next stop is called Queen's Bath and is located inside the high class neighborhood of Princeville, where most houses go for at least $200,000 or more.

Queen's Bath is one of the most unique and refreshing swimming areas on the island. This natural "pool" is carved into a lava shelf and is the size of several large swimming pools. When the surf is cooperating, usually in the summer months, the water is calm and crystal clear. However, if the surf is pounding you likely won't even be able to find the pool. The government will occasionally close this site during the winter months due to rough natural conditions. A small, freshwater stream flows nearby and is the perfect

place to rinse off after sunbathing and swimming in the bath. Views of the ocean and the rocky shoreline here are fantastic. Even when the surf is fairly calm, waves crash on the rocks shooting spray high into the air. Small fish and tiny sea life also call Queen's Bath home. After you are done enjoying the pool, walk around to some of the other inlets and look for honu (sea turtles). They graze on the algae on the sides of the lava.

To reach Queen's Bath, turn right on Ka Haku Road right before mile marker 28. Turn right on Punahele and right again on Kapiolani. Park along the road at the end of Kapiolani and follow the dirt trail along the stream for about 25 yards. At the end of the trail turn left for about 300 yards to the Bath. If you are here at sunset you'll be in for quite a sight. The views are absolutely breathtaking as the sun sinks below the horizon with nothing between you and Alaska to the north.

K A U A I
N O R T H

HANALEI VALLEY SCENIC LOOKOUT
Mile Marker 0 - Highway 560 (★★★★☆)

Our next stop is beautiful Hanalei, and it begins where Highway 56 ends and 560 begins. There are many folks who will refer to the whole northern part of Kaua'i as Hanalei. It's actually the name of a city, bay, beach, river, valley and lookout. The valley of Hanalei is a mile wide and 6 miles long and it is home to the Hanalei National Wildlife Refuge. The entire valley is surrounded by majestic mountains. An overlook provides an excellent view of the valley from above. This is our next stop.

After you turn back onto Highway 56 leaving Princeville, it'll be less than a mile to the overlook on your left. This is also the official location of the highway change from 56 to 560 at mile marker 0.

Hanalei Valley overlook is a picture waiting to be taken.

Hanalei's taro fields are a way to go back and visit the past. Taro was once the staple food crop of the Hawaiian people. It was used to make a purple paste called poi. Using a poi pounder the taro stem was mashed into the paste and then eaten. Today you can still taste poi in various places, but most people say it tastes like purple wall paper paste and root. Mmm-mmm, tasty.

The majority of all of Hawai'i's taro is grown here. Taro is used to make poi and numerous other food products that are the mainstay of many Hawaiians' diets. The fields are constantly irrigated with water and are grown in squares giving the valley a patchwork quilt look.

Beautiful, tall waterfalls flow down from the high mountains providing the valley with the abundant water needed to grow this crop.

HANALEI TOWN & HANALEI BAY
Highway 560 - Mile Marker 4 (★★★☆☆)

Hanalei is a leisurely little town situated on a beautiful crescent-shaped bay. The town is about as eclectic as it gets, everyone from surfer dudes to new-age folks call this place home.

To get to Hanalei after visiting the lookout at mile marker 0, you'll head west on Highway 560 and travel down into the valley on a graded road. At the bottom of the road is a one-lane rickety looking bridge. Don't let appearances fool you, it has been around for many years and is quite safe. It does, however, have a 15-ton weight limit. Since the bridge is one-lane, drivers must use bridge etiquette - all vehicles on one side cross together and then all vehicles on the other side cross.

Hanalei town offers good food, some shopping, and a chance to live the simple life.

Hanalei Bay is a magnificent crescent-shaped bay. If you are lucky enough to take a helicopter ride or hike the Alaka'i Swamp Trail, then you'll get to see this beautiful bay from above. Below is the view from the Kilohana Lookout on the Alaka'i Swamp Trail in Koke'e State Park (located in West Kaua'i above Waimea Canyon - see page 198.)

TUNNELS BEACH & REEF
Highway 560 - Mile Marker 8 (★★★★☆)

If you are looking to try your hand at snorkeling, this is a great place. It is such a supreme snorkeling location because it has a massive reef that is so large it can be seen from space. As can be seen on the following page, even the view from a helicopter is impressive and shows the magnitude of the reef. The waters are generally calm which also makes the beach popular for scuba divers. There is a slight rip current, but most of the time it is weak.

Two roads provide beach access, one 4/10 mile past mile marker 8 and the other 6/10 mile past mile marker 8 (the latter is the better of the two). Parking can be a hassle because you will have to park along the side of a narrow road. The

Tunnels Beach is not only great for snorkeling, it's great for photography as well. Check out the view.

roads are a bit hard to find, but there are a few signs placed by residents that let you clearly know which roads do NOT lead to Tunnels Beach. Please show aloha and don't park at those spots.

The beach itself is nearly directly across from mile marker 8 on Highway 560, but we highly recommend that you do NOT park on the street, the police will ticket you for doing so. Attempt to visit this spot earlier in the day so that you'll get a parking spot at the locations we mentioned above. There is one last spot available to park, but it requires some walking. Before the 8 mile marker is Alealea Street where parking is usually available near the sand. It's a half mile walk to Tunnels Beach (heading west) from here.

Also please keep in mind that like most north shore beaches, the conditions in the winter may, and likely will be, rougher than in the summer months.

LIMAHULI GARDEN & PRESERVE
Highway 560 - Mile Marker 9 (★★★★☆)

Past mile marker 9 on your left is one of the most fascinating gardens on the island, Limahuli Garden & Preserve. The 1000 acre garden is now part of the National Tropical Botanical Gardens after being donated to the society in 1976. In 1995, the garden was opened to the public and as of 1997 was rated by the American Horticultural Society as the best natural botanical garden in the United States. The garden, nestled in the mountains, is unique and a real treasure to visit.

One of the most amazing areas of the garden is the taro gardens and terrace system, the origins of which date back a century or more to the earliest Hawaiians. An overlook, as seen on the following page, allows you to get an amazing view of this archeological wonder.

Today, 17 acres of the garden and rain forest provide visitors a chance to view both the natural beauty of the island and the cultural history behind it. The garden is a great place to walk the land where taro still thrives on ancient lava rock terraces, learn about native plants of the Hawaiian chain, and become educated on the best environmental practices of water, soil, and rare plant conservation in the state of Hawai'i.

The garden is, as of press time, open Tuesday-Friday, and Sundays from 9:30 am until 4:00 pm. There are several guided tours available as well as self-guided tours. The cost is $15 a person for the guided tours and $10 for self-guided tours. Most people agree it's well worth the money, so if you have some time on the north shore, definitely stop by and visit this site.

This overlook of Limahuli Garden is an excellent way to view the terraces that were once used to grow taro to feed the Hawaiian people. These ruins are believed to be between 750-1000 years old.

Limahuli Stream also makes its way through the garden to the ocean. You may have noticed it on your way in. It's often used by visitors at Haʻena and Keʻe Beach to wash off sand and seawater from their equipment and even themselves after a dip in the ocean.

You can learn more about the garden, view photographs, and check for updates on their web site at:

www.ntbg.org/gardens/limahuli.html

WET/DRY CAVES & HA'ENA BEACH PARK
Highway 560 - Mile Marker 9 (★★★☆☆)

For our next stop we will explore two wet caves, a dry cave, and Ha'ena Beach Park.

Right after mile marker 9 you will notice a large dry cave (Manini-holo) on the left side of the road. You can park on the side of the road or in the parking area at Ha'ena Beach Park across the street. The cave goes back about 100-150 feet with plenty of standing room. After exploring the cave, you should cross the street and walk along Ha'ena Beach. It is not particularly good for swimming,

Waikanaloa Wet Cave

because it is not protected by a reef and the surf can be rough. It is, however, a nice place to get a shave ice from a local vendor.

You will find the two wet caves further down the road about half a mile after mile marker 9 on Highway 560. The caves, Waikapala'e and Waikanaloa, will be on the left side of the road. A short hike is required to reach Waikapala'e. These caves used to be sea caves which were formed by crashing waves when the sea was higher.

Manini-holo dry cave is the perfect place to explore an underground cavern while on Kaua'i. Here you can see the awesome power of the ocean over time. After exploring in the dark, you can lounge in the sun across the road at Ha'ena Beach Park.

KE'E BEACH STATE PARK
Mile Marker 10 – End of Highway 560 (★★★★★)

Our journey of the north shore ends at one of the most popular beaches on Kaua'i, Ke'e Beach. The beach marks the end of Highway 560 and the portion of Kaua'i that can be seen by car. The rest of north Kaua'i is occupied by the Na Pali Coast, a series of rugged seaside cliffs stretching along the northwest shore that is not navigable by vehicle. Parking is available on either side of the road and near the coast. We've seen Ke'e at many times of day, and it is equally crowded. Parking may be difficult, but usually is not too much of a problem.

Ke'e is very popular with snorkelers and families. One of the most striking aspects of this beach is its breathtaking view of the Na Pali Coast, which begins here. When you are facing the ocean, Na Pali can be glimpsed to your left. The best time for photographs is early morning (on a clear day) or right at sunset. The last time we were there, we saw a couple taking advantage of a gorgeous sunset to exchange their vows.

At the far end of the beach on the Na Pali side is a trail that winds through the jungle to an ancient Hawaiian heiau (temple), Ka-ulu-Paoa Heiau. This heiau has been used as a hula school for over 1,000 years.

Public rest rooms and showers are available at the beach. And though of no real value, the wild Kaua'i chickens that roost around the beach are entertaining to watch. How often do you see a chicken on the beach?

The famous Kalalau Trail also begins at Ke'e Beach.

K_AN O R T H_UA I

Our last stop in north Kaua'i is the end of the road, literally. Here you'll find beautiful Ke'e Beach, one of the most popular beaches on the entire island. One piece of advice, don't miss the best part of the beach. Sounds like a no-brainer, but it's really easy to do. The two photos above of Ke'e Beach are quite nice and make the beach a dream to visit... If you didn't know any better that was all you'd see. But Ke'e has a secret. Head down the beach to your right (as seen in the right photo above where the trees get thicker near the shore) and look back where you came from at the beach entrance, and viola... Na Pali in all its glory! The view at sunset is even better (see page 42).

KALALAU TRAIL
Mile Marker 10 – Highway 560 (★★★★★)

Starting at Ke'e Beach this 11-mile trail along the Na Pali Coast offers some of the most amazing ocean views along with lush vegetation and untamed waterfalls. Hiking the first two miles of the trail to Hanakapi'ai Beach is probably the easiest way to get a taste of what

Kalalau Trailhead

Kalalau has to offer without camping overnight. This trail is best attempted when dry as the mud can be very intimidating after a rain.

This is a good opportunity to warn you about Kaua'i's mud. Many companies have made a good business out of dying all

As you begin the trail and turn the first bend, you will be face to face with the hardest part of the trail, "the climb" as it's often called. Once you get to the top the trail levels off and is significantly easier to Hanakapi'ai Beach.

sorts of clothing using Kaua'i dirt. Do not wear any clothes or shoes that you are not willing to sacrifice to the red-staining power of the mud.

Because of the rocky and muddy terrain, sturdy hiking boots are recommended, but carry sandals in your backpack for crossing streams. It's extra weight, but it's better than wet feet rubbing in boots.

Now, back to the trail. The trail head is located at Ke'e Beach to the left of the parking areas. A covered sign board with maps and warnings provides useful information, as well as plenty of fliers asking people to keep an eye out for lost wedding rings and watches. The first half mile is fairly steep and rocky, so

NORTH KAUAI

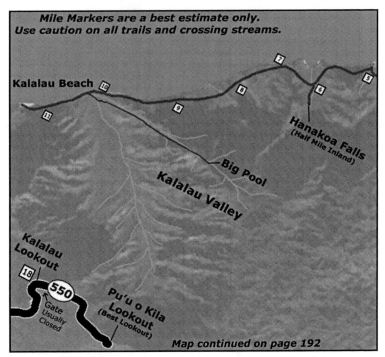

Mile Markers are a best estimate only.
Use caution on all trails and crossing streams.

Kalalau Beach

Hanakoa Falls
(Half Mile Inland)

Big Pool

Kalalau Valley

Kalalau Lookout

550

Gate Usually Closed

Pu'u o Kila Lookout
(Best Lookout)

Map continued on page 192

watch your step. Near the half mile mark you will get your first good look at the stunning Na Pali Coast stretching out ahead of you. Behind you will be Ke'e Beach. This view makes you appreciate just how high you've climbed on the trail. This is one of the premier photo spots on the trail, so be prepared to stop and snap a few photos. Make sure to soak in the beauty of the jungle plants and wild orchids along the way.

The last mile is full of switchbacks and is fairly steep, a hiking stick could be useful. You

Map continued on page 130

will be able to glimpse Hanakapi'ai Beach through the trees as you get closer. It will be necessary to cross a fairly deep and fast-flowing stream in order to reach the beach, but rope has been provided to help guide hikers across. The reward after crossing is well worth it, and we'll talk more on that at our next stop, Hanakapi'ai Beach.

A word of caution. If it has rained recently or looks like it is raining mauka (inland) you might want to consider not crossing until the stream slows down a bit and the water level

drops. It doesn't take long for a stream to rise or fall in Hawai'i, so keep that in mind and use caution.

There are two campgrounds and outhouse facilities at the entrance of the beach. The outhouse facilities are old, not serviced, and are often run down so be sure to prepare accordingly.

Nearing Hanakapi'ai Beach the views from the Kalalau Trail will both thrill and amaze you. This is truly hiking at its finest.

This Ke'e Beach overlook near the half-mile mark on the Kalalau Trail provides remarkable photo opportunities.

Hanakapi'ai Beach is usually the turn-around point for day hikers, and it is as far as we're going to take you here. A permit is required to hike past Hanakapi'ai and should you choose to continue along the trail, the next campsite is at four miles near Hanakoa Falls. From Hanakoa it is five miles to Kalalau Beach and campsite. The Kalalau Valley is immense, bordered on each side by green-draped cliffs. Native Hawaiians called this secluded area home until 1919. The valley can also be viewed from the Kalalau Lookout at the top of Waimea Canyon Drive. The trail beyond Hanakapi'ai to Kalalau is very difficult and has often earned the reputation as one of the hardest trails in the world. It can also be very dangerous at times as it skirts along the edge of cliffs. If you're up for a good adventure, then by all means make the journey, but for most folks Hanakapi'ai Beach and the trail inland to Hanakapi'ai Falls is just enough.

HANAKAPI'AI BEACH & FALLS
Kalalau Trail - Mile Marker 2 on Trail (★★★★☆)

After hiking two miles of rugged terrain you may be tempted to go for a swim at Hanakapi'ai Beach, but resist the urge. The waters are rough and the rip tide extremely dangerous. A sign is posted on the trail indicating how many hikers have lost their lives swimming at the beach. Instead, we recommend relaxing on the boulders or peeking inside the wet caves and leave the swimming for Ke'e Beach.

This aerial photograph of Hanakapi'ai Valley provides a bird's eye view of both the beach and the hike to Hanakapi'ai falls. The falls are nestled in the center of the photo between two ridges in the back of the valley.

Hanakapi'ai Falls is only two miles inland.

If you aren't too tired and have some time, consider taking a two-mile hike inland to see Hanakapi'ai Falls. The trail can be rough in spots, but the 300-ft waterfall at the end is worth the trek. Take notice of the native plant life as well as the small bamboo forests you will pass through. The trail crisscrosses the stream several times, so be mindful of water flow. Make sure to pack rain gear because showers pop up frequently and carry drinking water since it is not safe to drink stream water. Once you reach the falls feel free to reward yourself with a dip in the pool, just watch out for any falling rocks.

After you've seen Hanakapi'ai Beach/Falls it's time to make the trek back to Ke'e Beach. Give yourself about an hour for every mile you plan to hike. It's a four mile round-trip hike from Ke'e to Hanakapi'ai Beach, and a eight mile round-trip hike from Ke'e to Hanakapi'ai Falls. All said and done the hike from Ke'e to Hanakapi'ai Falls and back again takes about 8 hours (with ample time for photos, rest, etc).

K $\overset{SOUTH}{A}$ U A I

SOUTH KAUA'I - WEST LIHUE
Mile Marker 0 – Lihue on Highway 56 (★★☆☆☆)

If you've already completed the east and north areas of the island, you're likely already familiar with Lihue town and are now eager to make your way south and west. Last time we started from Lihue (page 100) so that the mile markers would count up as we headed north, so we'll do the same here again. When we head south and then west along Highway 50 the mile markers will count up as we go. But before we leave Lihue we'd like to introduce you to one place on Rice Street, the Kaua'i Museum.

Map continued on page 158

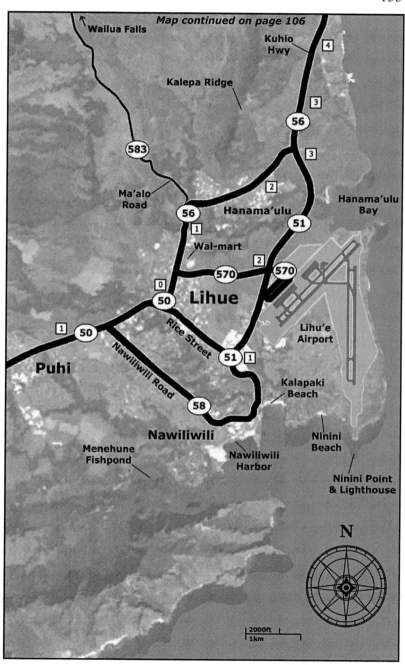

Map continued on page 106

Wailua Falls

Kuhio Hwy

4

Kalepa Ridge

3

56

583

3

Ma'alo Road

56

2

Hanama'ulu

Hanama'ulu Bay

1

51

Wal-mart

570

2

570

0

50

Lihue

Rice Street

Lihu'e Airport

50

1

Puhi

Nawiliwili Road

51

1

Kalapaki Beach

58

Ninini Beach

Nawiliwili

Menehune Fishpond

Nawiliwili Harbor

Ninini Point & Lighthouse

N

2000ft
1km

THE KAUAʻI MUSEUM
Mile Marker 0 – Highway 50 (Rice St) (★★★★★)

At the Kauaʻi Museum on Rice Street you will find an interesting variety of Hawaiian artifacts, displays, and information on the history of the island. There is a gift shop as well in which you can purchase maps, books, and other souvenirs to remember your visit by. Admission to the museum is only $7.00 and may prove both a fun and interesting activity on a spare day of your journey or one in which the weather didn't cooperate with your plans.

If any of your plans include hikes or camping that require permits, you can find those government buildings directly behind the museum on Eiwa Street.

OK, now we're set to begin heading south along Highway 50. Our first stop, Tree Tunnel.

TREE TUNNEL
Maluhia Road - Off Highway 50 (★★★☆☆)

To reach our next destination you must take Highway 50 west out of Lihu'e. We will take a short trip south to explore some of the sights in Po'ipu. Three quarters of a mile past mile marker 6 take a left on to Highway 520 or Maluhia

Road. One of the first sights to greet you is Tree Tunnel. In the early 1900's, a wealthy Scottish man, Walter Duncan McBryde, donated all the extra eucalyptus trees he bought to landscape his estate, some 500, to be planted here. There are fewer trees now due to road construction, but it is still a fascinating drive. The trees used to intertwine high above the road before two hurricanes damaged the tree tops. The best place to photograph the tunnel is right at the start of Maluhia Road near Highway 50. About halfway past mile marker three Maluhia Road will dead end into Koloa Road

in the town of Koloa. It is a quaint little town with a few shops and places to eat. It is worth a quick stop to explore. If you turn left, the road leads to a residential area. Turning right leads you to our next stop.

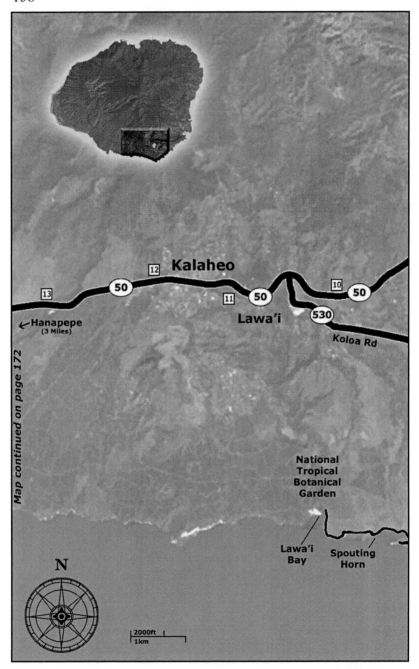

Map continued on page 172

Kalaheo

50

12

13

50

11

50

10

←Hanapepe
(3 Miles)

Lawaʻi

530

Koloa Rd

National
Tropical
Botanical
Garden

Lawaʻi
Bay

Spouting
Horn

N

2000ft
1km

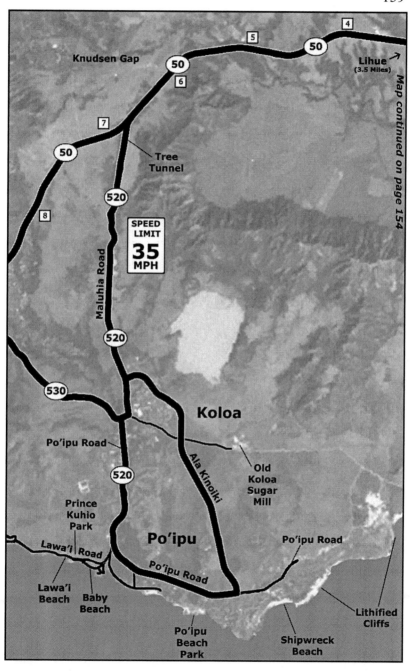

Knudsen Gap

Tree Tunnel

SPEED LIMIT **35** MPH

Maluhia Road

Koloa

Po'ipu Road

Old Koloa Sugar Mill

Ala Kinoiki

Prince Kuhio Park

Po'ipu

Po'ipu Road

Lawa'i Road

Lawa'i Beach

Baby Beach

Po'ipu Road

Po'ipu Beach Park

Shipwreck Beach

Lithified Cliffs

Lihue
(3.5 Miles)

Map continued on page 154

K SOUTH AUAI

PRINCE KUHIO PARK
Lawa'i Road - Off Po'ipu Road (★★☆☆☆)

After a brief visit in Koloa turn left onto Po'ipu Road from Koloa Road. The road will wind slightly past the Kiahuna Golf Course. At around mile marker 5 Po'ipu Road will branch off to the left. Follow the right fork onto Lawa'i Road with goes along the coastline.

Prince Kuhio Park is less than a mile on your right. The park is a monument to Prince Jonah Kuhio Kalanianaole who was raised in Koloa. Had Hawai'i not been annexed to the United States, he likely would have reigned as king. Instead he was elected as a congressional delegate for Hawai'i for 10 consecutive terms.

He was known as a tireless champion of Hawaiian culture and is so beloved that his birthday, March 26, is a state holiday. The foundation of his home and fishpond are protected in the park. It is very well maintained with a pleasant view of the ocean.

Parking is available to the left in the back. Besides an ocean view, the park is home to the Ho'ai Heiau. It sits on the left side of the park and is an exquisite example of stone construction. Its lava stones are so well-fitted that they almost appear to be carved (see photo above).

K A U A I
SOUTH

SPOUTING HORN BEACH PARK
Lawa'i Road - Off Po'ipu Road (★★★★☆)

After leaving Prince Kuhio Park, take a right and continue on Lawa'i Road. About a mile down the road on the left is Spouting Horn Beach Park.

The ocean attraction can be viewed from the top of a small hill with a guard-rail. This is a popular spot for tour buses, so expect to share some space at the rail. Like other blowholes, Spouting Horn is caused by a hole in a lava shelf. The ocean rushes under the shelf and up through the hole with a mighty force that sends water shooting into the air. What makes this blowhole slightly different is the addition of a second hole that only emits wind and creates a great moaning sound.

Spouting Horn is one of the highlights of south Kaua'i and unlike blowholes on other islands, it is right beside the road.

At first glance you might think there was nothing located at the Spouting Horn overlook. But within a few moments water erupts into the air like a volcano displaying the power of the hidden blowhole.

Spouting Horn puts on quite a show at high tide but is equally entertaining most of the time. It is possible, although not encouraged, to go beyond the guard-rail and explore the lava bench. This activity is done at your own risk as some unfortunate souls have been injured or killed when a large wave sucked them into the blowhole.

There are rest rooms in the park. It seems that this area is also popular with local merchants who will set up booths of souvenirs. If you have some time, be sure to take a second to peruse your way through their booths. You might just find a treasure worth taking home.

K A̅ U̅ A I
SOUTH

NATIONAL TROPICAL BOTANICAL GARDEN
End of Lawaʻi Road - Off Poʻipu Road (★★★☆☆)

At the end of Lawaʻi Road is one of the most magnificent gardens on Kauaʻi, the National Tropical Botanical Garden. It is actually two gardens in one: the 252-acre McBryde Gardens and the 100-acre Allerton Gardens.

The Allerton Gardens were once a private estate and are full of fountains, lush greenery, and interesting flowers. It is also home to the famous Moreton Bay fig trees that were featured in the movie *Jurassic Park*. If you can remember the scene were Dr. Alan Grant and the kids discover the dinosaurs eggs, well, that's the tree. Below is a photograph of this magnificent plant.

A large fig tree as seen in the movie 'Jurassic Park.'

Tours of the garden are guided and normally last two hours. The fee is $30 and reservations are required. Visitors must check in at the Visitors Center across the street from Spouting Horn Beach Park.

The McBryde Gardens are adjacent to the Allerton Gardens and are home to the world's largest collection of native Hawaiian flora. The tours are not guided and reservations are not required. The fee is $15 for the 1-1.5 hour tour. A tram leaves for the garden from the Visitors Center.

To contact the gardens, you can call 808-742-2623 or visit their web site at:

www.ntbg.org

K A U A I
SOUTH

PO'IPU BEACH PARK
Off Po'ipu Road (★★★☆☆)

From the National Tropical Botanical Gardens we're going to head east over to Po'ipu Beach. To get to the beach you'll take Lawa'i Road east back toward Po'ipu for about 2 miles. Lawa'i Road will merge with Po'ipu Road. You want to turn right onto Po'ipu Road continuing to head east. Right beyond the Po'ipu Shopping Village (which will be on your left) there will be a road named Hoowili Road on your right. This is the road that provides beach access.

Po'ipu Beach is one of the most popular beaches in south Kaua'i. Its three crescent-shaped strips of sand

Po'ipu Beach borders along another beautiful beach, Kiahuna Beach. Together they make up one of the most beautiful stretches of coastal scenery on the island of Kaua'i.

Po'ipu Beach is a world renowned beach and has made the Travel Channel's list of America's Top 10 Beaches. We also included it in our top 5 beaches of Kaua'i, ranking it in at number three.

offer a variety of swimming possibilities. For the more experienced swimmer, the edges of the crescents offer snorkeling and boogie boarding opportunities. The younger or inexperienced swimmer can stay towards the middle where there is a lifeguard on duty.

Kaua'i is renowned for its beautiful beaches, and Po'ipu is no exception. It was ranked at the top of the Travel Channel's America's 10 Best Beaches. In addition to spectacular scenery, Po'ipu Beach also provides showers, rest rooms, and picnic tables.

SHIPWRECK BEACH
Near end of Po'ipu Road (★★★☆☆)

From Po'ipu Road take a right into the parking lot between the Hyatt Regency Kaua'i and the Po'ipu Bay Resort Golf Course. From here, a trail provides access to Shipwreck Beach and the lithified cliffs beyond it.

Shipwreck Beach was named for an old wooden shipwreck that could once be seen offshore. It has since disappeared. The hills surrounding the far eastern portion of the beach are all lithified sand dunes. They are commonly referred to as the Makawehi Point Cliffs, our next stop.

We do want to advise you that swimming at this beach is unsafe and at times dangerous. Strong rip currents, high

The Makawehi Point Cliffs or Lithified Cliffs are an extra treat at the far eastern edge of Shipwreck Beach.

surf, and gusty winds create conditions that are hazardous to swimmers. Please keep in mind that even if you see locals using the beach for swimming, they have a lot more experience with those conditions than you do. The beach is in fact a popular spot for local boogie boarders, windsurfers, and body surfers.

K A U A I
S O U T H

LITHIFIED CLIFFS OF MAKAWEHI
End of Po'ipu Road (★★★☆☆)

Located next to Shipwreck Beach, these ancient limestone sea cliffs have been virtually sandblasted by a combination of wind, salt and water over millions of years. Lithified cliffs form as weathered fragments are removed by erosion and transported by gravity, running water, glaciers, waves, and wind. These weathered rock fragments then eventually come to rest as layers of loose, unconsolidated material called sediment. This material may subsequently be subjected to compaction and cementation, causing it to be lithified into solid rock. Sediment is lithified when it is compacted by the weight of overlying layers and cemented as percolating ground water fills pores with mineral matter.

It's hard to imagine that these ancient lithified cliffs on Kaua'i owe their presence to the last ice age.

When sea levels drop, these cliffs are exposed as we see them today at Makawehi.

This entire particular stretch of Kaua'i's coastline is also a treasure trove of fossils, petroglyphs, and burial grounds. The numerous fossils in the sand can also be explained by the lithified cliffs as they formed under water. As fish and other organisms died they would fall on top of the sediment layers and eventually be covered up by new layers. This allows them to be preserved as the fossils we find in the sand today. Please do not remove these fossils from the cliffs and sand so that others may also enjoy them. This area is considered particularly sacred and valuable to both locals and conservationists.

172

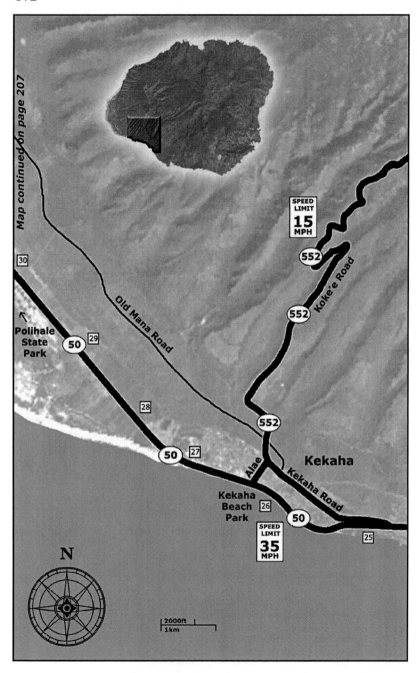

Map continued on page 207

SPEED
LIMIT
15
MPH

552

Koke'e Road

30

Old Mana Road

552

Polihale
State
Park

50 29

28

552

Kekaha

50 27

Alae

Kekaha Road

50 26

Kekaha
Beach
Park

SPEED
LIMIT
35
MPH

25

N

2000ft
1km

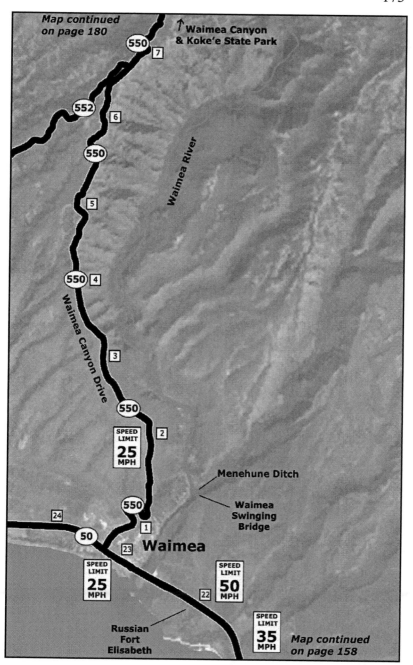

Map continued on page 180

↑ **Waimea Canyon & Koke'e State Park**

550
7

552
6

550

5

550 4

3

Waimea River

Waimea Canyon Drive

550

2

SPEED LIMIT
25 MPH

550

1

Menehune Ditch

Waimea Swinging Bridge

24

50

23 **Waimea**

SPEED LIMIT
25 MPH

SPEED LIMIT
50 MPH

22

SPEED LIMIT
35 MPH

Russian Fort Elisabeth

Map continued on page 158

K A U A I
W E S T

WEST KAUA'I - RUSSIAN FORT ELISABETH
Mile Marker 22 – Hwy 50 (★☆☆☆☆☆)

To reach the next spot take Po'ipu Road north to Koloa Road. Take a right on Koloa Road and then a left onto Highway 520. Highway 520 will terminate at Highway 50, take a left and continue west. There isn't much to see for about the next 15 miles. You will pass through the small towns of 'Ele'ele and Hanapepe, but there is not a lot in these towns to justify a stop, unless you have a few minutes to spare for exploring.

Just past mile marker 22 is the old Russian Fort Elisabeth which dates back to 1816. It was built by George Scheffer, an unscrupulous man who was employed by a Russian company. He built the fort as part of a misguided plan to help King Kaumauli'i reclaim full power of the island

At first glance you might assume the ruins of this spot are an-other Hawaiian heiau, but a little reading at the diagram inside the park reveals it's actually an old Russian Fort from the early 1800's.

from the reigning King Kamehameha. The Russians found out about his plan and forced him to leave. There is little more here than piles of rocks where the stone foundation once stood.

There are several plaques detailing the whole story as well as a self-guided tour. Rest rooms are available inside the park.

K A U A I
WEST

WAIMEA TOWN & SWINGING BRIDGE
Mile Marker 23 – Hwy 50 (★☆☆☆☆)

When you exit Fort Elizabeth take a left onto Highway 50 and you will enter the town of Waimea. This small town is the very spot where Captain Cook first landed in the Hawaiian Islands in 1778. They have built a small statue in his honor. This is a good place to fill up the gas tank and grab a bite to eat before taking the trip up Waimea Canyon Drive.

Before you head up to the "Grand Canyon of the Pacific," take a right onto Menehune Road, just before mile marker 23. After driving for less than a mile through a neighborhood, you will spot the Waimea Swinging Bridge on your right. The bridge, a re-creation of the original one that was destroyed

Waimea town as seen by helicopter. The forbidden island of Ni'ihau is seen on the horizon in the distance.

Waimea Swinging Bridge has been recreated after the original was destroyed by Hurricane Iniki in 1992.

in 1992 by Hurricane Iniki, stretches across the Waimea River and provides access to farms on the other side. Pull over to the side of the road, walk across the street and check out the Menehune Ditch. At first glance it just looks like a ditch with a stone wall, but this structure has a lot of historical significance. It is rumored to have been built by Hawai'i's "little people," the Menehune, who arrived around 300 AD from the Marquesas Islands. Seven hundred years later the Tahitians would arrive and build the Hawaiian culture that is present today. The stones used to complete the ditch were brought from nearly six miles away. Some legends say it was even constructed in one night.

Now we'll head up Highway 550 along the Waimea Canyon Drive. To proceed turn mauka (inland) just beyond mile marker 23 on Highway 50.

K A U A I
WEST

WAIMEA CANYON DRIVE
Starting at Mile Marker 0 – Hwy 550 (★★★★★)

If there is one thing you must see on all of Kaua'i beyond the sights of the north coast, then let this be it, Waimea Canyon Drive. Along this road you will encounter Waimea Canyon, Koke'e State Park, Kalalau Overlook, numerous trails holding unimaginable treasures, and the highest rainforest swamp in the world, Alaka'i Swamp.

The highlight of the drive is undoubtedly Waimea Canyon. Dubbed "The Grand Canyon of the Pacific" by Mark Twain, Waimea Canyon is the largest canyon in the Pacific and truly a dramatic sight to behold. The canyon measures ten miles long, one mile wide, and more than 3,500-feet deep. It was carved thousands of years ago by rivers and floods that flowed from Mount Wai'ale'ale's summit. Today it is the home of the Waimea River, so named for the red hue of the

Waimea Canyon is a spectacle that should be seen by all means possible: by foot, by car, and definitely by air as seen in this photograph. The Waimea Canyon Drive runs along the top of the ridge.

water. In fact, Waimea means "red waters." The red tint is caused by several natural processes that are breaking down the ancient rock inside the gorge. Like the Grand Canyon in Arizona, through the process of weathering (precipitation), mass wasting (gravitational breakdown), and erosion (the river) the walls of Waimea Canyon are literally being rusted, broken down, and carried out to sea over time. From space, you can even see the tinted runoff making its way into the ocean.

Before you begin your journey up Highway 550 be sure to check your gas gauge. The round trip is about 36 miles with an elevation change of 4,000 feet.

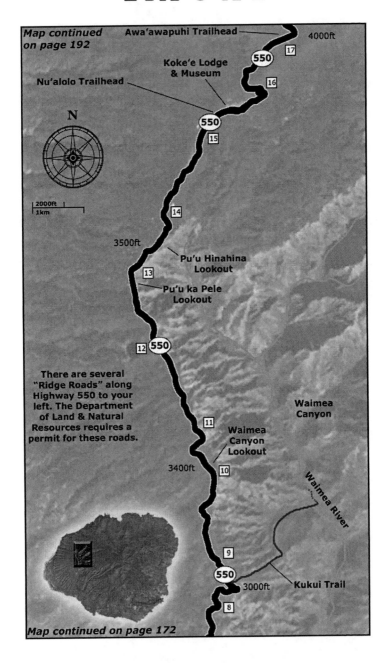

Map continued
on page 192

Awa'awapuhi Trailhead

4000ft

550

17

Koke'e Lodge
& Museum

16

Nu'alolo Trailhead

N

550

15

2000ft
1km

14

3500ft

Pu'u Hinahina
Lookout

13

Pu'u ka Pele
Lookout

12 550

There are several
"Ridge Roads" along
Highway 550 to your
left. The Department
of Land & Natural
Resources requires a
permit for these roads.

Waimea
Canyon

11

Waimea
Canyon
Lookout

3400ft

10

Waimea River

9

550

3000ft

Kukui Trail

8

Map continued on page 172

KUKUI TRAIL
Mile Marker 8 – Highway 550 (★★★☆☆)

As you begin your journey inland along Waimea Canyon Drive (Highway 550) it may surprise you how quickly the elevation changes. In fact, you are driving from sea level near Waimea Town to around 4,000 feet at the end of the Canyon Drive at Kalalau Lookout, an impressive elevation change in only 18 miles.

As you near mile marker 8, you'll pass above the 3,000-foot elevation mark and find the location of our next stop, the Kukui Trail. The trail starts on your right about 3/4 mile beyond mile marker 8. It is a steep but scenic trail down the west side of Waimea Canyon that drops 2200 feet in elevation over the course of 2.5 miles, ending at Wiliwili campsite on the canyon floor.

The Kukui Trailhead marker past mile marker 8

K A U A I
W E S T

Kukui Trail offers some absolutely gorgeous views of Waimea Canyon. The first part of the trail descends sharply, switch backing through the forest at first and then out in the open along the side of the mountain. You will be rewarded with some excellent views into Waimea Canyon along this part of the trail. For the most part, the trail is fairly narrow but still wide enough to comfortably accommodate hikers in single file. However, expect the trail to become extremely narrow in places, as little as eight inches wide on slippery dirt with nothing on one side of you. It's not really that dangerous, but just be careful and use good judgement when passing such areas.

As you continue down the trail, you'll come upon a huge stretch of slanted red rock that goes down the mountain. This red rock is where Waimea River gets is name. 'Mea' means 'red' in Hawaiian and 'Wai' means 'water,' so thus you have "Red Waters" as the meaning for Waimea.

KWESTAUAI

After traversing the red rock segment of the path, you'll descend deep into the forest where kukui nut trees grow in abundance earning the trail its name. As you descend deeper, you'll find yourself amidst waist-high grasses and passing huge spear-like plants. Not far below you is the Waimea River, and if you make the final hike to the bottom, make sure to look up and reflect on just how far down you've hiked, over 2,000 feet.

Once you reach the bottom, be sure to take a long rest. You'll need it before turning around to ascend the two miles back up to the rim. Remember to take it slow and easy and drink lots of water.

Once you're back at the trailhead, head further north along Highway 550 and explore the canyon from another point of view, the Waimea Canyon Lookout - no hiking required.

WAIMEA CANYON LOOKOUT
Mile Marker 10 – Hwy 550 (★★★★★)

Just beyond mile marker 10 at around 3,400 feet is the first overlook of Waimea Canyon, the official lookout maintained as part of Koke'e State Park. (Some say Waimea is its own state park, but the county says it's all part of Koke'e State Park.) This lookout has two levels which offer many stunning views of the canyon.

As a general rule of thumb, the official lookout is one of the best for viewing the canyon. However, we should note that there are still several lookouts ahead of you that offer distinctly different views from what you may see at the official lookout. Next we'll look at the Pu'u Ka Pele and Pu'u Hinahina Lookouts.

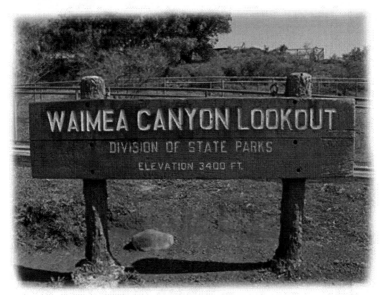

Just past mile marker 10 is our first overlook, Waimea Canyon Lookout. A short path leads to the viewing point.

Waimea Canyon - "Grand Canyon of the Pacific"

-Mark Twain

PU'U KA PELE LOOKOUT
Mile Marker 12 – Hwy 550 (★★★☆☆)

The first overlook we recommend visiting after Waimea Canyon Lookout is Pu'u Ka Pele. It is located shortly before mile marker 13 on the right side of the road. Occasionally the parking for this lookout is roped off, so you may have to park on the other side of the road and walk back over to see it.

The view into the canyon from this vantage point is unique to any of the other lookouts. The floor of the canyon literally drops away at your feet and you can get one of the best views of Waipo'o Falls available.

Pu'u Ka Pele lookout is often overlooked by visitors, but the views of Waipo'o Falls (in the upper right hand corner) are perhaps the finest from this vantage point.

PU'U HINAHINA & NI'IHAU LOOKOUT
Mile Marker 12 – Hwy 550 (★★★★☆)

Less than a mile up the road between mile markers 13 and 14 is the large Pu'u Hinahina Lookout. The viewing area perched above the jagged crumbling slopes looks straight down the head of another gorge. Hundreds of colors paint the canyon walls like a masterpiece of the natural world. More than any other, two colors are mixed

At around 3,400 feet above sea level Pu'u Hinahina Lookout is a good way to view Waimea Canyon. If you look to the right you can see all the way down the canyon to where the Waimea River meets the ocean in Waimea Town.

in different proportions as the day goes on. By the evening, one side glows with crimson highlights, the other basks in shades of dark green.

To the right of the same parking lot at Pu'u Hinahina is the Ni'ihau Lookout. If you are lucky enough to be here on a fairly clear day you should be able to make out the cloud-shrouded island of Ni'ihau. It's flat against the ocean with a large plateau, so it is not always an easy find. Directly to the island's right is the tiny pyramid-shaped island, Lehua. You can read more about Ni'ihau on page 29.

After leaving the Pu'u Hinahina lookout you may notice the Makaha Ridge Road off to your left. The road drops 2,000 feet over a relatively short distance to the Makaha Ridge Tracking Station in conjunction with the Pacific Missile Range Facility (PMRF) owned by the US military. If you

It takes a really clear day and good vision to make it out, but in the midst of the blue ocean is the small island of Ni'ihau beside the smaller island of Lehua.

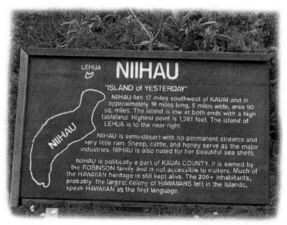

drive the road, use a low gear and watch your brakes. Also, while we're on the subject of military property, it's probably not a bad idea to point out that a lot of the Waimea area is in fact part of the PMRF and stretches all the way to near Polihale. You may notice the occasional radar or Doppler dish perched on a ridge or a gated fence blocking off a road in this area, but don't be alarmed, there's nothing to be worried about. At the end of Makaha Ridge Road, off to your left, there is an area for picnicking and some short hikes.

By now you may also have noticed that several "ridge roads" extend off to the left of the highway. These are primarily hunter's roads and all require a permit for driving, plus they are only open on weekends. If you absolutely must travel down them, we advise you to do so by walking, not driving. It won't be an easy trek, but it is our opinion that the average rental shouldn't go trailblazing down these non-maintained dirt roads.

Our next official stop is between mile makers 15 and 16, the Koke'e Museum & Lodge.

KOKE'E MUSEUM & LODGE
Mile Marker 15 – Hwy 550 (★★★★☆)

As you reach midway between mile markers 15 and 16 you should see the Koke'e Museum & Lodge parking lot on your left. Parking is free and a stop here is a good time investment, especially if it's one of those days the weather just won't cooperate with you at the canyon. As we've said before, weather changes fast on Kaua'i, so if you're experiencing undesirable weather, head over to the lodge for a while before trying the overlooks again.

The museum has several interesting displays where you can learn more about the island, its geology, flora and fauna, and even its history. A few of our favorite displays are the three-dimensional figure of Waimea Canyon, the factoids on Wai'ale'ale including the rain gauge showing the record precipitation amounts, and the wall dedicated to

the tragic story of Hurricane Iniki which struck the island on September 11, 1992. Iniki (Hawaiian for Enid) formed from a tropical depression that moved in from the east. It gradually strengthened into a major hurricane and turned north, with its eye passing directly over the island of Kaua'i. Iniki caused over two billion dollars in damage and killed six people. Iniki was the most powerful hurricane to make landfall in Hawai'i since Hurricane Dot in 1959. The wall serves as a tribute to what the category three hurricane did to the island and proof that the Hawaiian people can survive and continue to thrive after such a horrible natural disaster.

If you have any questions about Waimea Canyon or Koke'e State Park, the museum is the place to ask. The staff here is very friendly and knowledgeable. If you're looking for a bite to eat, head next door to the Koke'e Lodge.

K A U A I
W E S T

KALALAU & PU'U O KILA LOOKOUTS
Mile Marker 18 & 19 – End of Hwy 550 (★★★★★)

Our next stop is the jaw-dropping Kalalau Lookout. This isn't just another canyon lookout, as many suspect. It's a view into the heart of the Kalalau Valley, one of the most photographed and well recognized valleys in all of Hawai'i. This is primarily because the valley and surrounding coast have served as the backdrop for countless films including *King Kong* (the original), *Mighty Joe Young*, *Jurassic Park*, and *Six Days Seven Nights*. Even more remarkable is that the best lookout is one mile beyond this lookout at Pu'u o Kila. So why don't we just take you there instead? Well, as you may notice on the map below, it is because occasionally the road between

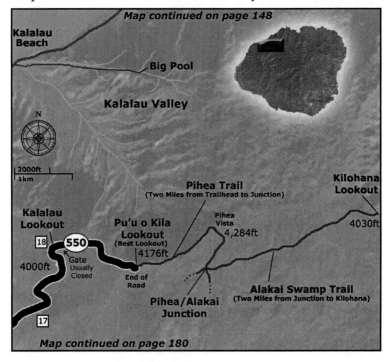

Map continued on page 148

Kalalau
Beach

Big Pool

Kalalau Valley

N

2000ft
1km

Pihea Trail
(Two Miles from Trailhead to Junction)

Kilohana
Lookout

Kalalau
Lookout

Pu'u o Kila
Lookout
(Best Lookout)
4176ft

Pihea
Vista
4,284ft

4030ft

18 550

4000ft

Gate
Usually
Closed

End of
Road

Alakai Swamp Trail
(Two Miles from Junction to Kilohana)

Pihea/Alakai
Junction

17

Map continued on page 180

the Kalalau Lookout and the Pu'u o Kila Lookout is closed off by the gate between the lookouts. In fact, the last two visits we had there it was closed both times. The road between is often pot-holed and crumbling, but even when it is in such condition we've never understood why the entire road is closed. If it IS open when you arrive, by all means make the drive to the second lookout a mile ahead as the views are even more incredible than the Kalalau Lookout. If not, Kalalau will be the only lookout available without some hiking. More on that in a bit.

Kalalau Lookout is also the highest elevation most people reach in Kaua'i by road, 4,000 feet. As we mentioned before, here you will find one of the greatest views in all of Hawai'i. Kalalau Valley is the largest valley on the island at two miles wide. Amazingly, it was inhabited up until 1919. Today the only way to visit the beach or valley is by the Kalalau Trail as it stretches 11 grueling

K^{WEST}AUAI

miles along the Na Pali coastline (see page 146). From this vantage point though you can just bask in the view of all that is between you and the blue hues of the Pacific Ocean.

We have found that the best time to view the valley is before 11 AM, as clouds are constantly moving in and out of the valley and are especially thick in the afternoon and evening. However, you also don't want to get there too early because the valley won't have full sun on it until around 8 AM most mornings (seasonal changes apply of course). Compare the photo above with the photo on the previous page to get a good idea of just how dramatically the sun can change the valley's appearance. If you arrive to a cloudy or mist-filled valley, consider the direction of the trades when you arrive. If the wind is blowing from the land towards the ocean, the clouds will usually enter the valley and fall (thus disappearing into the warm air below). However, if the wind is blowing from the ocean inland, the clouds will bank up

KAUAI

inside the valley and not dissipate but rather thicken into cloud soup. So keep that in mind during your visit.

Now, back to details on Pu'u o Kila Lookout. As we already mentioned, if the road is open between the lookouts, then just skip Kalalau and head straight for Pu'u o Kila. If it's closed, then you can settle for Kalalau or park near the gate and head out on foot over the road to Pu'u o Kila. Trust us, it's worth it. No photo can describe the difference in any way, shape, or form. However we're willing to try. The following two pages are all photos taken at the Pu'u o Kila lookout, so we hope that they will convince you to make the short one-mile hike if the gate is closed. Also, if you're here on a day of good weather, that two-mile round trip might be the best walk you ever make. We've visited on back-to-back days and the difference can sometimes be astounding. Don't always assume you can come back the next day and it will be the same.

The Hawaiian Goose, or Nene, is also a frequent visitor of the two overlooks.

If you take one "hike" on Kaua'i then let the one-mile trek between Kalalau Lookout and Pu'u o Kila be it. The expansive views of Kalalau Valley cannot be truly appreciated until you are standing before the cliffs of Pu'u o Kila.

From Pu'u o Kila Lookout you might not think it, but the further you move to the right, the more you'll discover. The shot below shows Kalalau Valley as seen from near the start of the Pihea Trail.

K A U A I
WEST

PIHEA & ALAKA'I TRAIL TO KILOHANA
Pu'u o Kila Lookout – End of Hwy 550 (★★★★☆)

After witnessing the Kalalau Valley from the two overlooks one might wonder if there was anything better left to see on Kaua'i. Admittedly, it is hard to find anything that can top the beauty of Kalalau, but our next hike might just be the thing, Pihea Trail.

Pihea Trail begins at the far right edge of the Pu'u o Kila Lookout and for the first few miles is right on the edge of the back Kalalau Valley rim. The views into the valley only get better and better as you continue further on the trail, until finally, as if Mother Nature has decided to no longer overwhelm your visual senses, you begin the march inland towards Pihea Vista and the Alaka'i Swamp Trail junction (see map on page 192). The scenery drastically changes from open valley to rainforest as you head into Alaka'i Swamp, the world's highest rainforest and swampland fed

Pihea Trail has a habit of creating "unique" trail situations in the first half of the hike. It's not as bad as it looks though, and a good hiking pole makes it all that much easier.

by the abundant precipitation on Wai'ale'ale's slopes. The trail is said to be the highlight of many visitors' journeys to the island, and it's one of our favorite hidden gems as well. As a bonus, in the last few years the trail has been greatly enhanced with boardwalks. No longer do hikers have to trudge through the mud to reach the magical lookout of Kilohana at the end of the journey. The hike is a total of 8 miles round trip, or 10 if you have to start from the Kalalau Lookout. This is a fairly easy day hike if you start early enough, and it's not overly strenuous. We highly recommend that all folks who are interested in hiking partake of this experience. Even if the view of Kilohana Lookout at the end of the trail is poor, the trail itself is a mystical journey through old Hawai'i.

The Alaka'i Swamp is the world's highest wetland "swamp" at over 4,000 feet above sea level. It doesn't feel like your average swamp though, the temperature averages around 70 degrees at best.

At the beginning, Pihea Trail skirts along the Kalalau Valley passing through forest of Ohi'a trees, ferns, koa, and other native vegetation. This is an excellent place to bird watch if time allows, you might even catch a glimpse of the 'I'iwi, a gorgeous red bird. It is medium-sized with a curved peach bill. As you finish the first mile of the trail (or second if you started from the Kalalau Lookout) a short but extremely steep side trail leads to the Pihea Vista. It's pretty, but it's not worth the effort, especially since you've only just begun the trail. Beyond this point, the Pihea Trail is covered mostly with boardwalk, as seen on the following page.

After approximately two miles on the Pihea Trail, you will come to a junction between the Pihea Trail and the Alaka'i

The Pihea & Alaka'i Swamp Trails have been much improved with the use of boardwalks. The previous trails were so thick with mud they were almost impassible. Below is the junction of the trails at two miles in.

Swamp Trail. You will want to take the path leading left on the Alaka'i Swamp Trail portion of the boardwalk (see photo on previous page). The last time we hiked the trail the remnants of old telephone poles still were present along the Alaka'i Swamp portion of the trail, the first being visible as soon as you turn left onto the Alaka'i Trail from Pihea.

From the junction to Kilohana Lookout it is about another two miles. The trail can be deceptive. Just when you think you are there, the swamp opens up again and the trail extends out for another few hundred yards. This is probably the hardest part of the hike (mentally because it teases you time and time again). Physically speaking, it's actually a fairly moderate hike, mainly because of the boardwalk. Without it you'd likely have already turned around and started back. The military had one heck of a time trying to get their phone lines placed here in World War II. Just imagine what hiking without the boardwalk would be like. The telephone

poles were put in place after the attack on Pearl Harbor as a means of backup communication in case the Japanese attacked and captured Lihue. It was the only successful passage of anything man-made through the swamp until the boardwalk was built in the late 1990's. The large open swath that is the start of the Pihea Trail was the first attempt at a road, but that idea quickly disappeared for what we're sure were countless reasons.

There is one small creek crossing that requires a fairly steep descent followed by an equally steep ascent back up to the trail. Other than that, it was easy enough. The only other bad part of the hike is the first part of the Pihea Trail. It can be "interesting" at times (see photo on page 199). The boardwalk is all easy enough, except for the steep portions of the stairs, but at least it's not a hill of mud climbing. We thought photos would show the extent of the stairs and steps involved, but it's not even close. The oddest part of the

The Alaka'i Swamp Trail is actually a pretty moderate trail, easy by some standards providing it's mostly boardwalk. But the never ending sight of wooden planks can leave even the most optimistic person asking, "When does this thing end?" Don't worry, it's all worth it!

hike is how one minute you're out in the open (see bottom left of previous page) and the next you're back in dense forest growth (like the photo on the previous page). Finally, the boardwalk ends at Kilohana Lookout. This is the point when it all becomes worth the effort as the views at Kilohana (seen above) stretch all the way from Ha'ena to Hanalei Bay. It's hard to believe that in ancient times the Hawaiians wouldn't stop here, but would actually continue over and down the 3,400 foot cliff. They would hike to the valley floor and then continue onward to the ocean. All of this was done to visit family when the north coast surf wouldn't allow passage by the shore in the winter. Talk about some serious trailblazing.

This is one of the best hikes on the island and if nothing else, certainly one of the most unique with its mix of vegetation and great scenery.

After Pihea/Alaka'i Swamp Trail there likely won't be a lot of energy left in you to hike. However, if there is, Koke'e State Park has one of the largest collections of trails in the entire state. We have only suggested our favorite spots here. The remaining trails we'll leave you to discover on your own. Maps are available in the Koke'e Museum and Lodge, and you can also see the most popular trails denoted on our maps. We can almost certainly assure you, however, that our selection of trails (Kukui, Pihea, and Alaka'i) are the highlights of hiking in Koke'e State Park. If we were asked what would follow we'd say, in order: Nu'alolo Trail, Nu'alolo Cliff Trail, and Awa'awapuhi Trail. For the really adventurous hiker, doing all three in a single day would be a real achievement, as the three are connected. We would advise doing them in the order listed and then hiking back down to your car from Awa'awapuhi Trailhead. Perhaps in future editions of this guide we'll include these trails. For now, we hope our trails have quenched your thirst for hiking.

Our journey now takes a turn back down Waimea Canyon Drive to the junction between Highway 550 and Highway 552 between mile markers 7 and 6. Highway 552 will be located on the right side of the road coming down from Koke'e. At the end of Highway 552 you will intersect Highway 50 again as it leaves Waimea on the far western side of town. Waimea Canyon Plaza is here if you wish to do any shopping. Our next stops will be back along Highway 50 heading west towards Polihale. So when you reach the intersection of Highway 50 and 552 simply turn right onto the highway to continue. (Note: You can also drive directly through Waimea to this point along Highway 50.) The map on page 172 may also be of help in navigating this stretch.

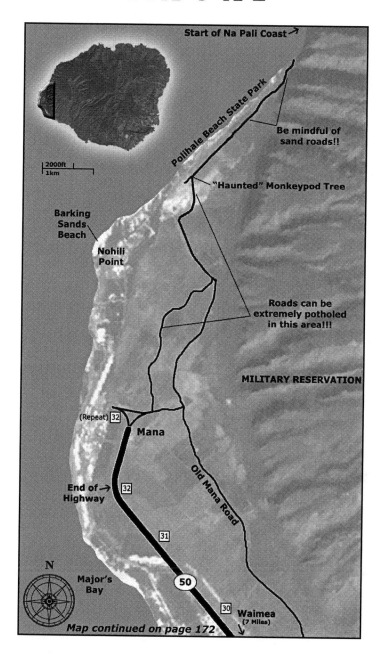

Start of Na Pali Coast ↗

Polihale Beach State Park

Be mindful of
sand roads!!

"Haunted" Monkeypod Tree

2000ft
1km

Barking
Sands
Beach

Nohili
Point

Roads can be
extremely potholed
in this area!!!

MILITARY RESERVATION

(Repeat) 32

Mana

Old Mana Road

End of →
Highway   32

31

N

Major's
Bay

50

30   Waimea
(7 Miles)

Map continued on page 172 ↓

K A U A I
W E S T

POLIHALE BEACH STATE PARK
Mile Marker 32 - End of Highway 50 (★★★★☆)

The road to Polihale may seem a little less like a tropical island and a little more like a desert highway. On a bright sunny day the flat stretch of Highway 50 between Highway 552 and Polihale Beach can create a mirage that looks more suited to Arizona than Hawai'i.

Near mile marker 30 take a look to your left and observe the high security of the Pacific Missile Range Facility (yet another thing that isn't quite so "tropical"). Once you pass mile marker 32, the highway ends and you will have to take a right inland. The first road on your left will take you to Polihale. Be warned, this is no pleasure ride in a small

Heading towards Polihale Beach you'll seriously start to wonder if you've entered another dimension. Mirages often flash before your vehicle as you drive this desolate area.

If the county hasn't recently smoothed the road, this stretch can be a nightmare for rental cars. Take it slow and watch out for bad ruts, and you should be fine.

vehicle. The drive is a long, bumpy sand road which can be a bear in a normal car. Fragments of front bumpers are strewn along the road as testament to motorists who were ill–prepared for some deep ditches. Keep your eyes on the road, and you should be fine. After a little over three miles, the road ends at a massive monkeypod tree which is rumored to be haunted. One local tale is that the ghost of a man who was hung there haunts the tree.

By now you're probably like, "Hmm, bad roads, mirages, and haunted trees... why are we going here again?" Trust us, it's worth the trek, just look at what's next.

KAUAI
W E S T

Polihale Beach dramatically ends where the Na Pali Coast begins.
The views are beautiful and yet strangely eerie at the same time.

After you reach the monkeypod tree bear right and drive until you see an area where a lot of other rental cars are parked. Then it is just a short hike up the dunes to the breathtaking vastness of Polihale. On the right are the majestic cliffs of Na Pali and to the left in the distance is the forbidden island of Ni'ihau. The pristine sands of Polihale can sometimes form 100-foot dunes. Local residents will drive their trucks and SUVs right onto the beach for camping or lounging. We advise you not try the same with your rental unless you have a 4x4. We've seen several people get caught in the sand in regular rental cars, and this is not a place you want to get stuck. Polihale, which is joined with Barking Sands Beach, is 17 miles long, which makes it the longest beach in Hawai'i. This is the end of the line on Kaua'i, as far as you can go by car.

The photo below shows the expansive view of the beaches as seen by helicopter, while the photo on the previous page shows the dramatic end of the Kaua'i coastline and the beginning of the Na Pali cliffs. The cliffs stretch all the way around the island back to the north shore at Ke'e Beach. If the weather is cooperating, this is a good location to also catch a glimpse of Ni'ihau on the horizon. The views from the Ni'ihau Lookout (page 187) on Waimea Canyon Drive are good, but we've found the best view from this beach. It's probably as close as you'll ever come to the forbidden shores of the island (see page 29).

Polihale is a mysterious place. Local legends say that the sheer cliffs at the end of Polihale are the "jumping off" place for all spirits that have entered Po, or the underworld.

Polihale Beach as seen from the air. Only from this vantage point can you truly appreciate the size of the beach.

Polihale has sort of a spooky feeling to it as the clouds swirl above the beach in strange movements, creating a tingling sensation through your body. Knowing the legend that Polihale is a place where spirits leapt to the underworld only heightens the effect.

Swimming here can be dangerous because the beach is unprotected. Rip currents are strong and the surf can be quite rough. The only safe swimming portion of the beach is left of the monkeypod tree heading towards Barking Sands. It is a portion of beach encircled by a reef known as Queen's Pond. Campsites are available here (by government permit), as well as picnic tables, rest rooms, and water suitable for drinking.

If time allows, also head over to Barking Sands Beach. If you're lucky, you'll discover why the beach is named as such while walking along the dunes.

END NOTES

Being from the southern United States, Kaua'i is not an island we were always familiar with. For many years the island was but a small and distant spec of land, the far western island in our nation's fiftieth state. Kaua'i is all too often misjudged because of its solitude in the island chain, often ignored because of its size and quiet atmosphere. It is hardly comparable to the size of the Big Island of Hawai'i and leaves much to be desired for those who seek night life, high rise buildings, and the urban atmosphere found on 'Oahu. But as small as the island is, and quiet though it may be, a lot of people have already seen Kaua'i, at least in part.

Kaua'i has been featured in dozens upon dozens of movies, films, and television shows. Chances are you've seen at least one show or film displaying the majestic Na Pali

K END NOTES I
KAUAI

cliffs on the island of Kaua'i. It was perhaps these scenes that first opened our own eyes to this amazing, yet simple place known only as 'The Garden Isle.' Kaua'i is a place of both unimaginable wonder and beauty. The vast majority of the island is truly a remote paradise waiting to be discovered and explored. What to many appears to be little more than a green dot of land on a map is quickly discovered to be the closest thing on earth to the Garden of Eden itself.

An island born of fire in the depths of the world's largest ocean some 5.1 million years ago, Kaua'i has embraced and sustained life of all kinds and all forms. It was here, in the most isolated place on the earth that Kaua'i evolved into a natural wonder unlike any other place on the planet. The rare birds and flora that lived upon the island became unique to the Hawaiian chain. When the first humans discovered the island it was here they too merged their lives, their culture, and their souls with the 'aina (land) of Kaua'i. Perhaps they unknowingly added to the magic and wonder that has become this mystical place. A land already graced by the presence of uniquely adapted flora and fauna would also soon birth the race of man we today call the "Hawaiians." The earth 'spoke' to these Hawaiians, and they listened – a system of life was born that remains famous for its chanting, mele (song), hula, language, kapu system, genealogy, and more. Today you can visit Kaua'i to vacation, but you'll leave with a greater appreciation for life, the 'aina, and the world as you know it. Kaua'i is in many ways a home to our souls, a place where we can truly feel at peace with the planet we live on. Perhaps it is the legendary power of the island we feel when we visit her lush shores, a force the Hawaiians often called mana, the life force. Perhaps it is the power of the mana that makes us feel both whole and pure, at peace with ourselves and our lives.

K *END NOTES* I
KAUAI

When you gaze off the edge of the Puʻu o Kila Lookout and survey the vast beauty of the Kalalau Valley, you can't help but feel a special mana, energy that comes not only from the people that once called this valley home for many years but also from the awesome forces of nature that carved its rugged cliffs. Or you could also stand on the edge of Polihale Beach and allow yourself to feel small in comparison to the massive Na Pali cliffs and envision the hundreds of years of legends that surround this place where earth so gloriously met water and created new land. The battle between earth and sea has long ensued in Hawaiʻi and still does to this day on the Big Island. But it was at one time here on Kauaʻi that Pele (the goddess of fire) and Kamapuaʻa (a demi-god of rain, moisture, and growing things) often dueled on these shores. Today, Kamapuaʻa's lush valley reigns supreme, but many hikers report to this day encounters with a beautiful woman on the Na Pali coast, all of whom swear the woman to be Pele herself. So she too returns home to this land from time to time making her peace with Kamapua'a in the lush valleys of Kaua'i.

While on your stay in Kaua'i do not let an opportunity pass you by to pause and reflect on these natural wonders and ancient legends. Let your worries slip away and truly appreciate what Kaua'i has prepared for you: the delicate scent of a plumeria blossom, the call of a zebra dove, the rustle of a breeze through a palm tree, or the gentle lullaby of the ocean waves.

All these things are the embodiment of Aloha. As we know, Aloha means so much more than just "hello" or "goodbye." It is a way of life, a spirit of love but also a connection to the earth that was here long before any human foot left an imprint.

If you do stumble across this feeling of Aloha, hold on to it and take it home. Let it guide you and remind you of the islands that reached deep inside and touched your soul. For the spirit of Hawai'i, the power of the mana, lives within us all. Kaua'i has a way of opening the mind's eye to that part of our being. The Garden Isle is full of hidden gems, but the greatest of all might be what you discover within... the treasure of your very soul. Hele on to Kaua'i and let the journey begin...

Aloha & A Hui Hou,

John & Natasha Derrick

The authors, John & Natasha Derrick, at Pu'u o Kila Lookout located at the end of Waimea Canyon Drive.

A Hui Hou

HAWAIIAN LANGUAGE GUIDE (CRASH COURSE)

The Hawaiian language is a dialect of the Polynesian tongue, other variations of which are spoken by Samoans, Tahitians, Marquesans, Tuamotuans and Maoris. The Hawaiian alphabet has only 12 letters: A, E, I, O, U, H, K, L, M, N, P, and W.

The vowels are pronounced:
A as in father, E as in vein, I as "ee" in peep, O as on own, and U as "oo" in boo.

The consonants are pronounced:
H as in hale, K as in Kate, L as in laid, M as in moon, N as in noon, P as in peak, and W as in always.

Rules of the Hawaiian Language:
Every word must end in a vowel.
Every consonant must be followed by at least one vowel.
Every syllable must end in a vowel.

BIBLIOGRAPHY & CREDITS

Aerial Photographs
National Aeronautics and Space Administration (NASA)
<http://www.nasa.gov/>

"Hawai'i." Encyclopædia Britannica. Encyclopædia Britannica Premium Service. 12 Jan. 2006 <http://www.britannica.com/eb/article-79280>.

GENERAL STATEMENTS

General Sightseeing
There are many locations on Kaua'i that are private property and we, to our best efforts, have attempted to avoid the use of such properties. It is our recommendation that all of our guide book readers avoid trespassing on Kaua'i lands when signs are clearly posted. Hawaiian Style Organization LLC takes no responsibility for the actions of its readers.

Dangers & Hazards
Kaua'i's paradise, make no mistake about it, but even paradise has its fair share of hazards. A few you should know about, in brief, are: Streams - don't underestimate the power of the streams/rivers in Hawai'i. One good rain, even far inland from where you are, can cause a stream to rise substantially. If you're crossing any streams or rock hopping, pay close attention to the weather and the water levels. The sun - A UV index of near 14+ every day speaks for itself. We recommend at least 15+ sunblock in Hawai'i at all times. Ocean life, plants, and animals - they're wild here too, so make sure you have respect for mother nature's creatures. There are a lot of plants and fruits you can eat alongside many trails in Hawai'i. Just make sure you've done your homework before biting into any mystery fruit. The ocean life and animals speak for themselves, don't become a statistic, be smart around wildlife.

Index

Remember Kaua'i year round with a beautiful 'Garden Isle' Wall Calendar

Get your own at:

www.HawaiianStyleMedia.com

Also Available...

...Or
these amazing color products:

*11x17"
photographic
prints,*

*15x19"
framed
pictures,*

*or 23x35"
satellite
posters!!*

Available only at:
www.HawaiianStylePhotos.com

Discover more of Hawai'i
Mile by Mile
on *Maui*

MAUI - Mile by Mile Guide
2nd edition

150 photos, 9 driving maps,
160 pages, detailed index, 5.25"x8.0"

Includes details on Hawaiian culture,
ecology, history, and more.

ISBN: 0-9773880-5-0 (Paperback)
ISBN: 0-9773880-7-7 (eBook)

www.HawaiianStyleMedia.com